This Man's Army

This Man's Army

A WAR IN FIFTY-ODD SONNETS

John Allan Wyeth

NEW INTRODUCTION BY DANA GIOIA

ANNOTATIONS BY B. J. OMANSON

THE UNIVERSITY OF SOUTH CAROLINA PRESS

Cloth edition published by Harold Vinal, Ltd., 1928
Paperback edition published by the University of South Carolina Press, Columbia, South Carolina 29208

www.sc.edu/uscpress

Manufactured in the United States of America

17 16 15 14 13 12 11 10 09 08   10 9 8 7 6 5 4 3 2 1

Library of Congress Cataloging-in-Publication Data

Wyeth, John Allan, 1894–1981.
  This man's army : a war in fifty-odd sonnets / John Allan Wyeth ; new introduction by Dana Gioia ; annotations by B. J. Omanson.
    p. cm. — (The Joseph M. Bruccoli Great War series)
  Originally published: New York : H. Vinal, 1928.
  ISBN 978-1-57003-779-5 (pbk : alk. paper)
  1. World War, 1914–1918—Poetry. I. Gioia, Dana. II. Omanson, B. J. (Bradley J.) III. Title. IV. Series.
PS3545.Y43T5 2008
811'.52—dc22

                                                            2008030221

I am indebted to the following people and institutions: Tad Bennicoff, Seeley G. Mudd Manuscript Library, Princeton University; Marisa Bourgoin, Corcoran Gallery of Art; Jo Cottingham, Interlibrary Loan Department, Thomas Cooper Library, University of South Carolina; Jacqueline Haun, Bunn Library, Lawrenceville School; Jessica Letizia, American Kennel Club Library; David Levesque, Ohrstrom Library, St. Paul's School; Princeton University Alumni Records; William Quirk, School of Law, University of South Carolina; Sandra Rosenstock, Firestone Library, Princeton University; Raymond Wemmlinger, Hampden-Booth Theatre Library; Garrick Davis, Mela Kirkpatrick, and Jon Parrish Peede, National Endowment for the Arts.

  Special thanks is also due to the Wyeth family, especially Ellie Wyeth, the poet's great-niece, who greatly assisted our research.

                                                        Dana Gioia

This book was printed on Glatfelter Natures, a recycled paper with 30 percent postconsumer waste content.

Contents

Series Editor's Preface

The Joseph M. Bruccoli Great War Series republishes fiction and personal narratives—the demarcation is not always clear—from the belligerent nations of World War I. Formal military history is excluded. "The war to end all wars" generated a vast literature—much of it antiheroic and antiwar. The best books of the war convey a sense of betrayal, loss, and disillusionment. Many of them now qualify as forgotten books, although they were admired in their time. The intention of this series is to rescue once-influential books that have been long out of print.

The volumes are drawn from the Joseph M. Bruccoli Great War Collection in the Thomas Cooper Library, University of South Carolina.* This collection is named for a private in the AEF who was severely wounded on the Western Front. Joseph M. Bruccoli's medal has eight battle bars, and he claimed that "they gypped me out of two battles." He was not embittered by his war.

M.J.B.

---

*The Joseph M. Bruccoli Great War Collection at the University of South Carolina: An Illustrated Catalogue, compiled by Elizabeth Sudduth (Columbia: University of South Carolina Press, 2005). See also The Joseph M. Bruccoli Great War Collection in the University of Virginia Library, compiled by Edmund Berkeley Jr. (Columbia: MJB, 1999).

Photograph of John Allan Wyeth. Courtesy of Ellie Wyeth; used with permission

The Unknown Soldier

An Introduction to the Poetry of John Allan Wyeth

I

John Allan Wyeth is the missing figure in the American literature of World War I—a soldier poet still worth reading. Little known in his own lifetime, he has been utterly forgotten by posterity. Even scholars and historians of the period don't recognize his name. Yet his work remains fresh and compelling eighty years after its publication. A graduate of Princeton and an acquaintance of Edmund Wilson and F. Scott Fitzgerald, Wyeth is an elusive, even mysterious character. Much of his adult life remains obscure. He left a surprisingly small paper trail for a writer who lived for nearly nine decades. His literary legacy consists of a single volume, *This Man's Army: A War in Fifty-Odd Sonnets* (1928). An innovative sonnet sequence that combines traditional and Modernist techniques, the book provides a vivid and historically accurate account of an American soldier's experience in the Great War. Most sonnet sequences bog down under the weight of their own formal machinery. *This Man's Army* moves with such steady assurance of style and purpose that it never loses either narrative flow or lyric impulse. A unique and original book, *This Man's Army* deserves a small but meaningful place in American literary history.

John Allan Wyeth, Jr., was born in New York City on October 24, 1894, the third and last child of Florence Nightingale Sims and John Allan Wyeth, Sr. The poet's father was a noted surgeon with a remarkable career that deeply influenced his namesake. Born in Alabama in 1845, the elder Wyeth served in the Confederate cavalry during the Civil War. Having volunteered at seventeen, he joined John Hunt Morgan's Confederate Raiders and was involved in several dangerous engagements, including Morgan's "Christmas Raid" of 1862. Taken prisoner in 1863, Wyeth was incarcerated at Camp Morton, Indiana, a brutal and undersupplied military prison, where thousands died and Wyeth himself suffered from measles, dysentery, pneumonia, typhoid, and malaria. When he finally reunited with his impoverished family in 1865, even his own mother did not recognize her ravaged son.

After taking a degree in medicine at the University of Louisville in 1869, Wyeth moved to New York for further study at Bellevue Hospital. In 1886 he married Florence Nightingale Sims, the daughter of Dr. James Marion Sims, a medical colleague, who had also come to New York from the South and had known Dr. Wyeth's father in Alabama. (A pioneer of women's medicine, Dr. Sims became so celebrated that he was memorialized in a statue in New York's Bryant Park.) Wyeth became a successful surgeon and important anatomical expert, but dissatisfied with the lack of advanced medical studies available, he founded New York's first postgraduate school of medicine, the New York Polyclinic in 1882. (Until then only undergraduate programs were available in medicine.) Dr. Wyeth was a widely published author in both medicine and history. His articles appeared in *Harper's* and *Century*. He also wrote poetry. In 1914 he published a celebrated memoir, *With Sabre and Scalpel: The Autobiography of a Soldier and Surgeon*. Florence Sims Wyeth died in 1915. Three years later the seventy-three-year-old Wyeth, still president of the Polyclinic Hospital, married the hospital's twenty-three-year-old dietician. He died in 1922 at the age of seventy-seven.

The young Wyeth grew up in a prosperous and cultivated household with a father who had distinguished himself as a soldier, author, poet, and surgeon. He attended the Lawrenceville School, a private preparatory academy in New Jersey, where he was president of the drama club and class poet. He published extensively in the *Lawrenceville Literary Magazine*. In 1908 a play by the thirteen-year-old author was produced as a charity benefit. In 1911 he entered Princeton University (from which his older brother had graduated in the class of 1910.) At Princeton Wyeth joined the Charter Club, one of the university's best "eating clubs." He studied mostly literature and languages, including Greek, Latin, French, Italian, and German. An average student, he graduated in the middle of his class (67th out of

115) but impressed his professors with his extensive knowledge of literature and personal charm. He contributed to the *Nassau Literary Magazine* and was a member of the Class Ode Committee. He graduated in 1915.

At first glance Wyeth's Princeton career seems typical of a gentleman scholar of his generation, but scrutinizing his records alongside those of his classmates, one notices an unusual pattern. Wyeth never had a roommate at Princeton, an odd arrangement on the compulsively gregarious campus. He also joined no teams or clubs, beyond his dining arrangement. One of his literary acquaintances at Princeton was Edmund Wilson (B.A., 1916), a fellow member of the Charter Club. Wilson once remarked that Wyeth was "the only aesthete of the Class of 1915." The remark obviously described Wyeth's passionate interest in the arts on a campus not conspicuous for its cultural enthusiasms. He was well-known by his classmates as a pianist and writer. But Wilson's coded term also suggested another way in which Wyeth differed from his classmates. He was almost certainly homosexual.

"Undecided about his future occupation," Wyeth taught high school French in Mesa, Arizona, for a year and then returned to Princeton for graduate study in Romance languages. By now his literary ambitions were clearer. He focused his energies on an academic career. Political events, however, intervened when the United States entered the Great War in 1917. Having completed his master's degree, Wyeth enlisted. On December 28, 1917, he entered the U.S. Army with the rank of a second lieutenant in the 33rd Division. His fluency in French secured him a position in the Interpreters Corps as part of the division headquarters staff. After training at Camp Logan in Houston, Texas, he transferred to Camp Upton in New York. On May 16, 1918, his division moved to Hoboken, New Jersey, where they boarded the USS *Mount Vernon* for France.

From this moment it is possible to follow Wyeth's wartime movements quite precisely because they form the substance of his sonnet sequence, *This Man's Army*. His poems are remarkably distinguished for specifically literary reasons, but they have the additional historical virtue of documentary exactitude. They chronicle the poet's journey through the war with a fidelity to circumstances more typical of nonfiction prose than lyric verse. Although no literary reader need note their accuracy, a military historian can rely on each sonnet to render the time, place, situation, even the weather. Likewise a literary critic or biographer can use them to illuminate the poet's military career.

Wyeth's army duties as a member of the general staff would have depended on the wishes of his commanding officers and the changing circumstances of the 33rd Division as it traveled. His primary role was to serve as French interpreter, a necessary and important task for an English-speaking American Expeditionary Force crossing through France and Belgium. But he would also have performed other assignments, many depicted in the sonnets, such as delivering messages and maps to the front lines by foot, car, motorcycle, and horse. (Some horses were still used by the general staff—a vestige of the traditional cavalry regiments of earlier wars—though motorcycles and cars mostly took their place.) At one point the speaker in Wyeth's poems, an overtly autobiographical figure, does sentry duty. As a member of the general staff, Wyeth would have been billeted close to headquarters, often a local chateau, but as a junior officer, he seems to have lived in more modest homes in nearby villages. These homes served as the settings for several poems.

Wyeth was discharged from the U.S. Army on October 23, 1919. He delayed his return to graduate school until the following year by claiming a "percentage of disability" to his obliging dean that required recuperation at his older brother's Palm Beach home. Wyeth returned to Princeton for the January term and then won a traveling fellowship to study for a year in Liège, Belgium, in pursuit of a doctorate. By 1923 he had finished his oral exams in French and German. At this point the academic paper trail stops until April 1926, when he applied to finish his doctoral studies, but his resolve proved short lived. In September Wyeth wrote from Rapallo, Italy, that he wished to drop his academic studies. "I have always desired above all things to try my hand at literature," he confessed to his graduate adviser, adding that he believed "that whatever literary talent I might come to possess could be brought into play in response to a complete wholehearted devotion to literary aims."

In his letter Wyeth states that his literary ambition "centered on the fictional creative side," but his address in Rapallo provides a possible clue why poetry would soon become his medium. The Italian seaside city's most famous American resident was Ezra Pound. Although there is no documentary evidence that Wyeth knew Pound (who moved from Paris to Rapallo in 1924), the English-speaking community was so small that it would have been unlikely for them to have missed one another. (Wyeth family members have confirmed the friendship.) It is impossible at this point to know what influence the older poet might have had on the wandering scholar, but one might reasonably speculate that Pound's example could have instigated or reinforced at least three significant decisions—Wyeth's break with academia for a literary career, his subsequent choice of poetry rather than fiction, and the selection of the Great War as the subject matter of his imaginative efforts.

The next two years in Wyeth's life remain a blank. Without any documentary evidence, a critic can only be silent or speculate. I will risk one crucial speculation. I believe that the poems in *This Man's Army* were not written until after Wyeth's arrival in Rapallo. The assumption seems likely for several reasons. First, there is no mention of the poems in any earlier document, not even his letter of withdrawal from graduate school. Second, in the same 1926 letter Wyeth suggested that his literary ambitions focused on writing fiction. Third, the sonnets in *This Man's Army* are so stylistically unified that they seem unlikely to have been composed over many years. Likewise their strictly narrative organization makes it implausible that they were written individually without any plan for the overall structure. Fourth, the poems have assimilated certain stylistic aspects of Modernism, especially its use of mixed meters and disjunctive syntax, which had not fully emerged until the 1920s in the works of T. S. Eliot, Archibald MacLeish, and Ezra Pound, all prominent American expatriates. Finally, the poems have a clarity of perspective and an emotional detachment that reflect an older and more mature man. Although the sonnet sequence unfolds in discrete chronological sections like a diary or journal, the controlled tone and steady narrative pacing suggest a distance from the events. One assumes—and in the absence of documentary evidence this can remain only an assumption—that the young Wyeth kept a detailed journal during the war that later served as the basis of his book.

Whatever its creative genesis, *This Man's Army: A War in Fifty-Odd Sonnets* appeared in late 1928 from Harold Vinal, Ltd., of New York City. A slim handsome quarto with a cubist dust jacket, the book bore a remarkably perceptive blurb by Morris William Croll of Princeton University. Labeled as "Extracts from a Critique," Professor Croll's comments still seem relevant and just:

> The problem was to put the image of the war-landscape, human character, dialect, glimpses of its personal sentiment, all that a novel does—put it into the defined form of verse and so convert it into beauty or delight. . . . In THIS MAN'S ARMY it seems to me that the problem is solved. The limits of sonnet-form are never transgressed. I mean, first, that the movement of the rhythm is always true sonnet-rhythm, and just as truly in apparently irregular passages, as the apparently regular ones; for the ear does actually hear the inevitable sonnet-beat even in passages imitating jazz-singing. And I mean, secondly, that the *drama* is always exactly moving towards its sonnet-completion and finality, however photographic the detail may seem to be.

This Man's Army received generally strong but brief coverage, mostly in omnibus reviews of recent poetry. The *Boston Globe* praised the "happy collection" stating that "Mr. Wyeth has been able to catch the elusive something which differentiates the poetic observation from the commonplace one." In the *New York Herald Tribune* Charles Divine considered the sonnet sequence "a series of pictures distinguished by their vitality and their graphic and emotional qualities." In the *Saturday Review of Literature* Edna Lou Walton awarded the volume only mild approbation remarking that it was "more about Mr. Wyeth than the war." In the *New Republic* "R.E.L." tersely delivered a mixed verdict, writing that "Mr. Wyeth's sonnets often achieve a sharp outline in one line, but the effect is dissipated by what follows." The *Boston Transcript* provided the longest and most favorable review, praising the volume's "dash and spirit" as well as its narrative structure:

> In a slim volume of fifty sonnets Mr. Wyeth has caught the color and drabness of the World War as seen through the eyes of the American soldier. He takes his readers through the shot

and shell of battles and to the still peaceful vales behind the lines. We eat corned willie and drink coffee in the mud-filled trenches of the ridge at Chipilly and open champagne bottles in the gay little cafes in Paris with the men on leave.

What particularly impressed the reviewers was Wyeth's innovative use of the sonnet form. There had been a broad revival of the sonnet in the Twenties—led mostly by female lyric poets such as Edna St. Vincent Millay, Sara Teasdale, and Elinor Wylie, as well as numerous others whose names have largely been forgotten, such as Jean Starr Untermeyer, Gladys Oaks, and Elizabeth J. Coatsworth. These poets represented a contrarian impulse to Modernist experimentation. Although sometimes bold in their subject matter they employed highly traditional prosody. The critics reviewing *This Man's Army* did not miss the pun on "odd" in the volume's subtitle. Nearly every critic remarked on Wyeth's novel employment of the form, including "rough dialogue," jazz music, tags from old songs, slang, and foreign languages, to achieve what the *Boston Transcript* termed "a colloquial ease which is most interesting and also technically correct."

Wyeth's small Vinal edition must have sold reasonably well since it was reprinted ten months later in September 1929, by Longmans, Green and Company in a trade edition. The timing could hardly have been worse. One month later the stock market crashed, the Great Depression began, and the cultural zeitgeist changed radically. The dynamic features of American literature during the Twenties— formal experimentation, cosmopolitan allegiances, iconoclastic perspective, irreverent satire—quickly shifted into the more earnest social and naturalist concerns of Thirties literature. Wyeth vanished from the literary scene. A few years later one last brief notice of his book belatedly appeared in *Poetry* (December 1932). It offered a mere forty-three words of interestingly qualified praise:

A group of sonnets, strung with slang and soldiers' *patois*, telling of the poet's experiences in the war. They are scrupulously exact description with little comment, and they ring with a vivid reality. They are probably not poetry, but they are good stuff.

There now occurred a seemingly unanticipated change in Wyeth's artistic interests. By the time the critical notice appeared in *Poetry*, the poet had decided to become a painter. In 1932 he began studying art with Duncan Grant, the Scottish painter and member of the Bloomsbury Group. He later worked for six years at the Académie Moderne in Paris under Jean Marchand, a French painter much admired by the Bloomsbury Group. Wyeth reportedly exhibited paintings in Paris during the 1930s, and he participated in three biennial Contemporary American Oil Painting group shows at Washington's Corcoran Gallery in 1939, 1941, and 1943. (None of the three paintings he exhibited was sold.) In 1939 he joined the Frank Rehn Gallery in New York, and by 1941 he was living back in his native Manhattan. He also served in the U.S. Coast Guard in World War II.

Wyeth's Post-Impressionistic landscapes were not conspicuously successful in the marketplace. Often relying on financial help from his family, Wyeth lived an itinerant existence in Europe and America. He spent some years in Providence, Rhode Island. The Princeton alumni organization consistently failed to locate him and eventually dropped him from the 1915 class roll "by mutual consent." He may also have become a Roman Catholic. By 1979 he had moved to a family house in Skillman, New Jersey. He died on May 11, 1981, at the age of eighty-six and was buried at the Blawenburg Cemetery. "John Allan Wyeth, noted area artist" read the headline in the short *Trenton Times* obituary. Neither of the two Princeton obituaries (nor the brief paid death notice in the *New York Times*) mentions his poetry.

II

Wyeth's poetic career began and ended with *This Man's Army*. Everything before the book was juvenilia. There seems to have been no verse published afterward. (One hopes that a trunk of unpublished manuscripts will appear in some relative's attic.) His poetic oeuvre consists of a single volume—with neither prelude nor coda. Moreover, his work made no lasting impression. Hardly noticed even when new, his poetry soon drifted into utter oblivion. With the exception of a brief biographical and critical note I published a few years ago and the inclusion of three poems in the anthology, *Twentieth-Century American Poetry* (2004), I co-edited with David Mason and

Meg Schoerke, Wyeth's work has never received critical or scholarly attention of any kind. His name and biography exist in no reference works. He is not mentioned in the many extensive critical works on the poetry of World War I—not even in the comprehensive studies by Paul Fussell, Jon Stallworthy, Patrick Quinn, or Mark Van Wienen. His work does not appear in any of the numerous anthologies of World War I poetry. Nor was he remembered or reprinted in anthologies of Princeton poets. His work, in fact, seem to have been reprinted only once in an obscure 1945 collection compiled by Mary Lou McDonough titled *Poet Physicians*, where it was mistakenly attributed to Wyeth's father. A relentless researcher will discover nothing in the literary record except a few sentences in Edmund Wilson's journals and F. Scott Fitzgerald's letters.

I must confess that no scholarly enterprise of my own led to rediscovering Wyeth. I first read his work in 1994 when poet and military historian Bradley Omanson asked my opinion on *This Man's Army*, which he had uncovered while researching the history of the American Expeditionary Force's 33rd Division. (Having discovered the poet in McDonough's anthology, Omanson believed that the book had been written by the elder Wyeth.)

I often receive copies of little-known or neglected books sent by people soliciting my advocacy for what they believe are worthy causes. Most forgotten books, however, do not merit renewed critical attention. Initially skeptical, I read *This Man's Army* with growing interest and excitement. It was not only a fine book but a unique one in American poetry. I was also confident that Wyeth was already known to scholars of World War I poetry. Few literary areas have been so intensely studied. It seemed unlikely scholars would have missed such a conspicuously excellent volume. Here I was mistaken.

I was also sure that Omanson was mistaken about the identity of the author. *This Man's Army* was not an old man's work. The elder Wyeth must have had a son and namesake. Indeed a little research among public records revealed the existence of the younger Wyeth. Although there was no scholarly record of his literary career, there were legal documents and school records. I tracked down a few family members who answered some questions and eventually provided an obituary. (Until then I did not even have the date of the younger

Wyeth's death—so slim was the documentary record.) There is obviously much more to be uncovered, but now at least there exists some context for *This Man's Army*, including some sense of who "this man" was.

III

World War I marked a decisive turning point in Western literature. The unprecedented scale of violence across Europe, the role of technology and science in accelerating the destruction, and the impotence of Western governments to avoid or even curb the conflict shattered the traditional notions of progress and civilization. Although the Modernist movement emerged before the Great War, it was in the bitter aftermath that it became the central artistic impulse of the age. World War I also transformed the notion of war poetry from battle pieces and inspirational odes to grimly realistic accounts of modern mechanized warfare.

Modern British poetry began in the bitter disillusionment and horrific experience of the soldier poets who fought in France and Belgium. Faced with a mechanized mass brutality for which traditional poetry had neither adequate language nor imagery, they were forced—by violence, loss, and suffering—to reinvent the art. The noble Georgian sentiments of Rupert Brooke were traumatically transformed into the stark modern idioms of Wilfred Owen, Siegfried Sassoon, T. E. Hulme, David Jones, and Isaac Rosenberg. Many of the "War Poets" were killed in battle, including Owen, Hulme, Rosenberg, Brooke, and Edward Thomas, but not before they had created a substantial and influential body of work. This tradition, which also included survivors such as Robert Graves, Edmund Blunden, and Ivor Gurney, occupies a crucial place in the history of modern British literature. For the British, Modernism began in the trenches of the Western Front.

By contrast, the American poetry of World War I has seemed either negligible or marginal. The work actually written by American soldier poets was mostly stiffly conventional—old language and attitudes dusted off to express a new situation. The two best known American soldier poets, Alan Seeger and Joyce Kilmer, both of whom were killed in action, brought a generalized and traditional approach that feels inadequate to the realities of modern mechanized warfare. In "Rouge Bouquet," for instance, Kilmer describes the mass death and dismemberment caused by artillery bombardment as follows:

> In a wood they call the Rouge Bouquet
> There is a new-made grave today
> Built by never a spade nor pick
> Yet covered with earth ten metres thick.
> There lie many fighting men,
> Dead in their youthful prime,
> Never to laugh or love again
> Nor taste the Summertime.
> For Death came flying through the air
> And stopped his flight at the dugout stair
> Touched his prey and left them there,
> Clay to clay.

Kilmer is trying to describe a horrific event, but his language, imagery, tone, and perspective fail him at every turn. (The poem gets worse as it proceeds.) Ultimately, the poem feels vague and euphemistic.

Alan Seeger's best poems, such as "I Have a Rendezvous with Death," are more effective, but they also eschew contemporary language and experience for traditional romantic archetypes:

> I have a rendezvous with Death
> At some disputed barricade,
> When Spring comes round with rustling shade
> And apple-blossoms fill the air—

In diction, imagery, and tone Seeger's poem, however memorable, could have been written about any earlier American war. He succeeds by describing a traditional notion of personal bravery in war rather than expressing what troops were actually experiencing in World War I. By personifying death as an individual, he also obscures the central horrifying reality of modern, mass warfare—it is no longer an enterprise in which personal combat or individual bravery much matters. The tragic inadequacy of traditional military and poetic rhetoric in the face of mass, industrialized slaughter was the hard lesson that the soldier poets had to tell the general public. Facing this challenge represented the difficult triumph of the British "Trench Poets." Avoiding it resulted in the failure of their American counterparts.

The best American poetry of World War I consists of a tiny canon written by noncombatants, such as Ezra Pound and E. E. Cummings, or by soldier poets, such as Archibald MacLeish or John Peale Bishop, who saw combat briefly but wrote only one or two poems about their experiences. (It was left to American novelists such as Ernest Hemingway and John Dos Passos to explore the wartime experience in depth.) The paucity of American war poetry—excluding the reams of patriotic or elegiac popular verse written at home—is not surprising. The United States was involved in the war for less than two years, and actual combat by American troops lasted only a few months.

Seen in the context of American and British World War I literature, the importance and singularity of Wyeth's *This Man's Army* becomes clearer. It is the most ambitious, representative, and successful poetic venture by an American combatant in the Great War, and it is also probably the only volume that stands comparison with the work of the best British soldier poets. *This Man's Army* is not a masterpiece. Its documentary and autobiographical narrative line abruptly ends at a crucial moment where a fictional work would have moved decisively to its climax. Yet the book remains powerful, authentic, and perfectly accomplished within its own terms. It is also innovative and original in its relation both to American war poetry and the sonnet form. Its rediscovery not only expands but alters the canon of American literature from the Great War. Wyeth's presentation of the specifically American war experience—violent but less tragic and traumatic than the longer, more brutally destructive Allied experiences—also provides a useful comparison to British war poetry.

This Man's Army is essentially a narrative poem told in isolated lyric moments. The strategy of breaking a linear narrative into disjunctive poetic moments is a mainstream Modernist technique, exemplified in such influential verse sequences as Pound's "Hugh Selwyn Mauberly" (1920). It is also a literary strategy that corresponds neatly to the older tradition of the European sonnet sequence, which characteristically tells a story through a series of heightened lyric moments. Wyeth's sequence, therefore, simultaneously fulfills the expectations of both a Modernist and a traditional poetic sequence—a tricky feat that adds to the book's enduring appeal.

What is particularly interesting about Wyeth's poetic treatment is that he brings such originality to both the lyric and the narrative elements. While one can easily compare *This Man's Army* in general terms to other long American narrative poems published at the same time, such as Robinson Jeffers's *Cawdor* (1928) or Joseph Moncure March's *The Wild Party* (1928), Wyeth's specific approach differs radically from those of his contemporaries. His lyric moments are tightly drawn in sonnet form, and the overall narrative remains detached and objective—indeed almost documentary in its careful and mostly dispassionate description—unlike the highly dramatic narratives of Jeffers and March. Although Wyeth's central subject of unrestrained modern war should equal or surpass the domestic violence in March or Jeffers, his narrative seems decidedly quieter and calmer. Although the book presents a first-person account of the first great modern war—a conflict generally depicted in literature through shock, horror, and confusion—the speaker seems to observe his own life from a safe distance. If Wilfred Owen declared that his poetry was "in the pity," Wyeth's method locates its imaginative energy in objectivity.

Wyeth's choice of the sonnet as his poetic unit may seem traditional, but his employment of the form is both experimental and idiosyncratic. No sonnets, before or after, resemble Wyeth's expertly handled measures. He invented a new rhyme scheme unlike any other in the form's seven-hundred-year history—*abcd abcd abe cde*. Wyeth also omits the traditional stanza breaks of the Petrarchan and Shakespearean form. The "turn" of each sonnet comes at different points as the theme or situation demands. With even greater boldness, Wyeth experiments metrically in the poems. He creates a system in which two different metrical systems coexist in the same poem—combining traditional lines of iambic pentameter with looser five-stress accentual lines. Often the conventional accentual-syllabic lines are used for narration and the stress meter lines employed for dialogue. In "Chipilly Ridge: Regimental Headquarters," for instance, the poem begins in iambic pentameter:

> Steep prickly slopes in shadow from the moon
> sagging behind us down the strident sky.
> Guns blaze and slam. The stars burn fever bright.
> A low white ridge ahead, and the crumpled sound
> of shelling.
>   "Jerry's out—"
>   A snarling croon
> wheels over us—quick glittering tracers fly
> down a pale searchlight, and along the ground
> bombs blast into smoky yellow shot with light. (36)

But as the battle breaks out and the narrator talks to his fellow soldiers, the verse shifts to the looser stress-based meter. This narrative moment corresponds to the "turn" in the traditional sonnet, which in this poem occurs precisely between octave and sextet—few of Wyeth's sonnets behave so conventionally. The lines now contain as many as thirteen syllables, though, with five identifiable stresses, and all lines still rhyme according to Wyeth's pattern:

> "These runners will get you up there pretty soon.
> —Take them up to the Second Battalion."
>   My tongue goes dry
> and scrapy, and my lips begin to jerk—
> —"Look out for the gas—they been pumping it in all night."
> "Let's go, Tommy."
>   "O God wait a minute—I've found
> something wrong with my mask—the damn thing doesn't work."
> (36)

Wyeth's innovations in the sonnet form go beyond prosody. Not only does he expertly mix meters, he also mixes languages. As French language liaison for the general staff, Wyeth crossed two linguistic communities. Both worlds meet in the poems. French vocabulary, dialogue, and quotations appear in the sonnets, usually without translation. Wyeth may have borrowed this macaronic technique from Pound and Eliot, though he minimizes Modernist disjunction by seamlessly weaving the French (and occasional German) into the metrical fabric and rhyme scheme. Wyeth also mixes high and low diction, as well as British and American military slang. He even recounts the soldiers' sometimes offensive jibes and jokes. *This Man's Army* ends—shades of *The Waste Land*—with a two-page "Glossary" of British and American military slang as well as French terms and idioms. Wyeth's omnivorous but oddly consistent reportorial style gives the poems both enormous acoustic variety and documentary authority. The genuine tone and texture of the war and its diverse combatants suffuse the sequence. This stylistic choice captures both the international nature of the war as well as the cultural dislocation of the AEF in its trek across Western Europe.

The narrative of *This Man's Army* is a journey into war. This sense of the narrative's momentum is never absent since the titles of the sonnets are mostly place names that document the army's progress town by town, village by village toward the German Hindenburg line. Although Wyeth's sequence portrays the same devastating battle-ground that the British Trench Poets depicted, his narrative reflects the less catastrophic American experience in the Great War. The United States declared war on Germany on April 6, 1917—nearly three years into the conflict. American divisions did not arrive in Europe until the spring of 1918, and there were not significant numbers of U.S. troops deployed until the summer. In essence the AEF fought only during the last nine months of the war—long after the colossal massacres at the Marne, Somme, Ypres, Verdun, and Passchendaele that transformed modern consciousness. The American forces, with fresh troops and ample supplies, faced an exhausted and wounded German army. Advancing through ruined countryside, the Americans encountered brutal combat but not the deadly stalemate of the previous years.

That historical situation is reflected in Wyeth's narrative. The landscape is ravaged, the combat is violent, individual soldiers are at risk, but the eventual American victory never seems in doubt. With each sonnet the soldiers move closer to the German lines toward the climactic battle, which never occurs in the book. Here the autobiographical nature of the poem undercuts its larger historical narrative. *This Man's Army* consists of fifty-five sonnets arranged in chronological order. In sonnet 53 the speaker is in Lempire examining the wreckage of a burnt German plane shot down in a dogfight. Suddenly in the next poem, the volume's penultimate sonnet, he is in a U.S. Army hospital in Souilly, where he is stricken with influenza. In the final poem the narrator is on a hospital train leaving the front. The closing lines of the sequence seem anticlimactic. There is neither a final battle nor a military victory, just an exchange between two sick soldiers:

> "Where was you wounded, Bud?"
> "Aw I'm not wounded Buddy—it's just the flu." (55)

However accurate in factual terms, Wyeth's ending is abrupt and unsatisfactory in narrative terms. There could be few duller ways to end a war poem. But Wyeth's deliberately unheroic conversation has an ominous side. The conversation depicted may take place in the final weeks of the war, but the poem was written some years later when it was clear that the worldwide influenza epidemic—spread by returning troops after the Armistice—would kill even more people than the Great War itself.

The cruel irony of the book's final lines provides a certain frisson, but overall the concluding sections of the poem feel inconclusive and anticlimactic. Wyeth's fidelity to the narrator's personal experience—which is presumably also the author's personal experience—prevents the book from achieving a broader resonance. As the early reviewer noted, the book is ultimately more about Wyeth than the war itself. The reader may long for an impersonal, even epic conclusion, but the author refuses to move beyond autobiography. *This Man's Army* is a strongly written, authentically detailed, and imaginatively engaging book that fails to reach its full poetic, historical, or cultural potential. Even as one savors the various qualities of this unique volume, one cannot help imagining the stronger book it might have been had Wyeth decided, like Hemingway, to fictionalize his personal material.

It is, however, useless to bemoan the book that might have been, especially when the volume that exists is so fine—as well as virtually unknown. The new edition of Wyeth's *This Man's Army* reclaims a

lost and singular work to the canon of American poetry. Its republi-
cation, after eighty years, meaningfully enlarges the literature of
World War I. There is no better book of poems about the American
experience in the Great War. The volume also lays claim to a small
but interesting place in the history of the sonnet. Not only are
Wyeth's form and style unique in the sonnet tradition, there are few
sonnet sequences that take war as their central subject. John Allan
Wyeth may have missed the opportunity of creating an epic poem,
but he managed to tell his own personal story so well that his poems
remain fresh, compelling, and human.

Front jacket of the 1928 edition of Wyeth's sonnets

Annotations

Note: Many of the details in these notes are drawn from Will Judy's A Soldier's Diary. Chief Army Field Clerk William L. Judy, like John Allan Wyeth, was a member of the 33rd Division's headquarters staff. He was often in the same place at the same time as Wyeth, and his diary records incidents referred to in Wyeth's sonnets.

To emphasize the geography of the 33rd Division's movement through the French countryside, the place-names associated with the poems have been foregrounded. The typographic layout of each poem supports such a reading although it is sometimes at odds with the order on the contents page.

Germany's Spring Offensives, 1918

On March 21, 1918, while Lieutenant John Allan Wyeth and most of the 33rd Division were still in preliminary training at Camp Logan, Texas, General Erich Ludendorff launched the first of five great offensives on the Western Front, designed to crush the British and French armies and win the war before sufficient numbers of fresh American troops could enter the fighting. The initial blow fell on the Somme front, on the Fifth British Army, recently weakened by the fighting at Passchendaele. Within a week the Germans advanced forty miles along a fifty-mile front, and by April 5 they had taken Bapaume, Albert, Peronne, Montdidier, and Noyon and were within a few miles, and easy artillery range, of the crucial railway hub of Amiens. The danger loomed of a breakthrough to the sea, with the capture of the channel ports and separation of the British and French armies.

On April 9 Ludendorff set loose a second offensive against the British, capturing Armentières, but stopping just short of Ypres and Bethune. The British line wavered but did not break, and by late

April Ludendorff accepted that he could not achieve his breakthrough in the north.

On May 27 Ludendorff unleashed his third great offensive, this time against the French. Once again, initial successes were overwhelming. Within a week Soissons fell and the Germans steamrolled as far south as Chateau-Thierry, where they stood on the banks of the Marne, forty-five miles from Paris, the key to victory.

Camp Upton: Sailing Orders

May 15. Wyeth's "sonnet-narrative" opens at the conclusion of his stateside training. Assigned to Headquarters Detachment, 33rd Division, as the divisional interpreter, Wyeth began his military career on January 3, 1918, at Camp Logan, Texas. At the completion of training, the division moved to Camp Upton, New York, for final preparations prior to sailing overseas. Special Order No 124, the "sailing orders" of the sonnet's title, specifies that divisional headquarters, together with other divisional units, is to leave Camp Upton for Hoboken, New Jersey, on May 16, there to board the USS *Mt. Vernon* for departure to France.

Camp Upton to Hoboken: Secret Troop Movement

The early hours of May 16. The sonnet opens in the station yard at Camp Upton, where Wyeth and his comrades are boarding a troop train. They pull out at 3:30 A.M., arriving in New York City at 6 A.M.; they ferry across to Hoboken and march to Pier 5, arriving at 8 A.M. Within the hour Wyeth and four thousand other soldiers have boarded the USS *Mt. Vernon*. At sunset the ship steams from New York Harbor.

The Transport: I

Night, May 22–23, on board the USS Mt. Vernon.

The Transport: II

The evening of May 23.

Brest: The Waterway

May 24. Judy's *A Soldier's Diary* notes, "We crowded the decks, shouted, laughed and sang; here was France, our eyes saw the goal of our adventure; we had outwitted the submarine; the lure and romance of France were just ahead" (84).

Brest: The Waterfront

May 24 or 25. Brest's waterfront, "the scourge of the provost-marshal," has the worst reputation of all the French ports. Its attractions include the Rue de Siam with its "regiments of streetwalkers" and a high incidence of bar fights among sailors (Stallings, *The Doughboys,* 175). Doughboys are diverted from the waterfront altogether, being marched to departing trains or to nearby Pontanezen Barracks. Officers are at liberty to explore the waterfront.

The Train from Brest

May 25–26. Wyeth's train pulls out of Brest at 3:20 on the afternoon of May 25 and arrives in Paris at 4:30 in the morning of May 26— a grueling thirteen-hour journey over a distance of some six hundred kilometers.

On to Paris

May 26. The division commander has orders to proceed from Paris to Rouen, but on their arrival at the Gare Montparnasse, the Americans are met by a British staff officer who carries orders changing their destination to Oisemont. Lieutenant Wyeth is instructed to take his men by the metro to the Gare du Nord, where they will board a train to the north.

The British Front

May 26. By midday Wyeth's train has traveled some eighty-five kilometers north-northwest from Paris to Beauvais, where the poem opens. In or near Beauvais, the Americans change trains and continue northwest for another seventy kilometers or so, arriving at Oisemont in the evening. It is here, for the first time, that they are able to hear the rumbling of artillery.

Oisemont: Place de la Mairie

The evening of May 26.

Oisemont: British Detraining Station

The night of May 26–27. In the poet's mind it is already June, but he is a few days ahead of himself. With the dawn will come orders to move again, this time ten kilometers north to Huppy.

Huppy

May 31. Headquarters for the 33rd Division is established at Huppy on the afternoon of May 31. The division is designated part of the American Army II Corps and passes to the jurisdiction of the Fourth British Army. The divisional history records, "A course of intensive training was immediately inaugurated" (Huidekoper, *History of the 33rd Division,* 1:35).

With nightfall the Americans hear German bombers over Abbeville, ten kilometers to the north—close enough to raise alarms in Huppy. These raids are a nightly affair. The divisional history records, "At this time the town of Abbeville was so severely bombed almost every night by enemy aeroplanes that slow evacuation was begun. The German preparation for their anticipated drive to the sea via Amiens and Abbeville was apparently well underway" (Huidekoper, *History of the 33rd Division,* 1:35).

Huppy: The Life o' Riley

Night, after 9 P.M., sometime between June 1 and June 8. Wyeth and several of his chums are on a carouse. They find a café and walk in past the protesting proprietress, who tells them that the café is closed, at which one of them replies, "Allez toot sweet ('tout de suite' means right away) to hell." A soldier orders Black and White brand scotch. The proprietress obliges. A soldier launches into "You're in the Army Now," a very popular anonymous song of the war.

Eu

June 9. The 33rd Division begins moving, in two marches, to the Eu area, where it is to replace the 35th Division AEF. Headquarters detachment, including Wyeth, moves from Huppy to Eu on June 11, a distance of some thirty kilometers. In the Eu area, the division undertakes a program of intensive training, prescribed by General Headquarters, AEF, and assisted by the British 30th Division.

Eu: Interior

Miscommunication between nationalities, especially the mangling of the French language by American soldiers, was, as often as not, deliberate.

Le Tréport: The Seashore

Judy describes this nearby seaside resort in *A Soldier's Diary*: "Spent the afternoon at Tréport, two miles away, a pretty place on the English channel, about midway between Calais and Havre, and directly south of the far southeastern coast of England. Both the Americans and English have hospitals on the high stone cliffs overlooking the sea" (98).

Eu to Molliens-au-Bois: Motor Convoy

June 21. The sonnet opens at the town square, in Eu, at 8:30 A.M. The trucks are British lorries, with a capacity of twenty men each, and there are thirty-seven of them, numbered consecutively on their side panels. The general order detailing their route that day no longer survives, but an officer of the 131st Infantry, who followed an hour later in a separate subgroup, recorded the following details:

> We crost the River Somme at Flixecourt, followed it to Picquigny, sighted the spire of the cathedral at Amiens, passed a hundred ammunition dumps, and saw Chinese repairing roads, Italians laboring on rail lines, and slightly disabled Canadian and Australian soldiers building bridges. (Judy, *A Soldier's Diary*, 99)

When the convoys pass through the town of Villers-Bocage, the men spot the cathedral of Amiens, some ten kilometers directly to the south. At that point they are just a few kilometers from their destination.

Molliens-au-Bois

"Beale Street Blues" by W. C. Handy was a national hit in the United States in 1916. When this and other ragtime / early jazz songs were first played to French audiences, the music caused a sensation.

Molliens-au-Bois: Regimental Concert

"Just a Baby's Prayer at Twilight" (1918), with music by M. K. Jerome and lyrics by Sam Lewis and Joe Young, was a very popular sentimental ballad recorded by Al Jolson.

"Livery Stable Blues," composed by Ray Lopez and Alcide Nunez and recorded by the Original Dixieland Jazz Band, was one of the hits of 1917 in the United States. It was frequently performed with animal sounds, which might explain the exception taken to it by the duke's horse.

"Wal, I Swan! (Giddap, Napoleon)" was a 1917 comic song by Benjamin Hapgood Burt.

Tramp comedians were popular vaudeville acts.

Molliens-au-Bois: Allies

"Mademoiselle from Armentières"—also known as "Hinky Dinky Parley Voo"—was probably the best-known song among the American and British troops. The composer and lyricist were never identified, but Canadian songwriter Gitz Rice was credited with putting together the formal version in 1915.

Molliens-au-Bois: Air Raid *and* Molliens-au-Bois: General Order

June 26–27. These two sonnets are linked, as they focus on a closely related series of events. The first sonnet describes a late-night air raid, which interrupts the poet's reading of his Virgil by candlelight. Judy records, "The ground shook with pain." In the second sonnet the conversation of the soldiers takes up the latest gossip regarding the "General Order" of the sonnet's title, which, in response to the casualties from the previous night's raid, instructs the men to dig deep holes in the floors of their tents. Judy describes the specifics of the order: "Today all of us are digging sleeping holes in the ground about two feet deep so that shrapnel, the many rough pieces of metal, scattering out of the exploding bomb, will sweep over us. A hit within fifty feet kills all. Beyond that, safety is in lying as low as possible" (Judy, *A Soldier's Diary*, 100).

Molliens-au-Bois: The Village Road

Sometime after sunset, June 27.

Molliens-au-Bois: British Squadrons

Evening, June 27. Wyeth converses with his French host, Raichlin, before planes pass overhead. Judy, billeted in the same village, notes in his diary: "Forty-one British airplanes flew in a group over the enemy's lines just before dusk" (*A Soldier's Diary*, 100).

Molliens-au-Bois: Alarums

Late evening, June 27. "Archies" are antiaircraft guns. The "beast" is a bomber (probably a Gotha, the largest of the German aircraft).

Molliens-au-Bois: Abri

Night of June 27. A "cave" is a cellar; an "abri" is a dugout or shelter. Wyeth, Raichlin, and Madame Raichlin take refuge from the bomber. Madame comforts Wyeth: "It's not so bad; I spread straw on the ground." She asks him whether he has seen Paris, and he replies, "Once, before the war." Raichlin remarks, "The Parisians could understand nothing of our dialect." He then says, "It is over, Madame. Let us go up. I am dead tired." But Madame is in no hurry to leave the safety of the cellar. She says, "What is there to do? There is nothing pressing, nothing that can't wait."

Molliens-au-Bois: Home Mail

Sometime between June 28 and June 31, on the grounds of the Chateau of Molliens. The soldiers of the division are receiving their mail, which has come up on ration carts from the quartermaster, who has collected the mailbags from the postmaster.

Molliens-au-Bois: The Old Army Game

Morning to midday, sometime between June 28 and June 31, 1918. The G-2's office in Molliens-au-Bois is the intelligence section; it also denotes the chief intelligence officer, which for the 33rd Division is

Major A. W. Copp. The G-2's assistant who answers the phone may be the 33rd Division's Captain Carl F. Lauer, First Lieutenant Evan A. Woodward, or First Lieutenant Robert J. Fisher.

In the wartime slang of the American Expeditionary Force, "the old Army game" means "passing the buck."

Molliens-au-Bois: New Diggings in the Orchard

Evening, sometime between June 28 and June 31. Wyeth has left his comfortable lodgings with the Raichlins and now sleeps on a cot in a dugout with a mud floor, stacked sandbag walls, and a sheet-iron roof. Because of continued air raids and the peril posed by flying shrapnel, headquarters has determined to get everyone as deep underground as possible.

Wyeth and his fellow officer are reading Lewis Carroll to one another by candlelight. It was, as Paul Fussell has noted, a very literary war, not only for Europeans but—if Wyeth and his companions are any indication—also for Americans.

The Attack on Hamel and Vaire Woods, July 4, 1918

In the first significant participation of American troops with forces of the British Empire, three Australian brigades under Lieutenant General John Monash, together with two infantry regiments (the 131st and 132nd) of the American 33rd Division, set out before dawn to capture Hamel and Vaire Woods south of the Somme for the purpose of strengthening British positions in front of Amiens, one of the key points along the Western Front. By 7 A.M. all objectives were taken, along with 1,472 German prisoners of war, 2 guns, 121 machine guns, and 26 mortars. The Australians suffered 775 casualties and the Americans 134 casualties.

In this first action by Americans on the British Front and the first combat action by the 33rd Division, the men of the 131st and 132nd regiments fought with noteworthy tenacity and courage, earning praise from British commanders Sir Henry Rawlinson and Sir Douglas Haig and from their immediate Australian commander, Sir John Monash.

Because Wyeth himself did not play a part in this action, no mention of it appears in his sonnets.

————

Molliens-au-Bois: Divisional Maneuvers

Date uncertain, possibly July 13. The troops are in the field, but the phone lines in the office of the G-2 are on the fritz, and no orders are getting through. The only calls getting through, apparently, are those from the commander of the division, General Bell, who is blistering Major Copp's ear.

Huidekoper's *The History of the 33rd Division* records a "division terrain exercise" at Molliens-au-Bois on several occasions, but always on days recorded as "clear" (2:317–18). One division-wide exercise takes place on July 13, a clear day followed by rain on the fourteenth.

The Tide of War Turns: Allied Counteroffensive, July 18–August 2, 1918

On July 18 the French 10th Army (including the American 1st and 2nd Divisions), supported by more than two hundred tanks and two thousand big guns, turned Ludendorff's fifth offensive ("Friedensturm") into a victorious Allied counteroffensive and, over the next seventeen days, retook Chateau-Thierry and Soissons and pushed the Germans back to the north bank of the Vesle River. Here the Germans dug in and stabilized their line. The tide of the war finally turned in favor of the Allies, but the costs to both sides were horrendous, with 95,000 French, 13,000 British, 12,000 American, and 165,000 German casualties.

————

Molliens-au-Bois: Concert by Elsie Janis

July 19. Elsie Janis, "the sweetheart of the AEF," was one of the famous vaudeville stars of her day. The first American celebrity to entertain American troops in a foreign war, she began her tour of the American front line sometime in the spring of 1918 and performed more or less continuously until shortly before the Armistice. Janis appeared according to hastily arranged schedules and frequently stopped to give impromptu concerts to small groups of soldiers she met along the way—as many as eight performances in a day, each in a different location.

The concert depicted in Wyeth's sonnet came at the end of a long, exhausting day. Janis had left Paris that morning at 9 A.M., stopped for lunch at Beauvais, and arrived at Abbeville at 5 P.M. Somewhere between Abbeville and Molliens-au-Bois, driving through rain and mud, her car had two flat tires, but she hitched a ride. During her rendition of "Darktown Strutters' Ball" (Shelton Brooks's 1918 hit song, which became a jazz standard), Janis was, in her own words, "leaping about festively" when the stage floor collapsed beneath her (*The Big Show*, 160). She fell through but managed to haul herself back up onto the stage. Immediately after the show, Janis was whisked to headquarters at a nearby chateau where nearly two thousand other doughboys of the 33rd, plus a couple of hundred British Tommies, were waiting for her on the chateau grounds. This is the setting for Wyeth's sonnet.

The "darky" story was standard material in vaudeville performances of the time, being an aspect of the blackface minstrel tradition that would persist on both the American and British popular musical stage until after World War II. Janis first heard the particular story contained in Wyeth's sonnet from an American officer in St. Nazaire, shortly after her arrival in France. It was subsequently repeated to her by other soldiers (usually African Americans) on at least ten occasions, and by the time Wyeth heard her in July, the story had become a regular part of her show.

Molliens-au-Bois: Machine Gun Emplacement

The story of the chance exhumation of a small horde of Roman coins by a soldier of the 132nd Infantry was evidently well known among members of the 33rd Division. *AUC: Ab Urbe Condita*, "From the founding of the city"; Æ S, "money or legal tender." Judy later wrote an essay about the discovery, which may have been published though no copy has been located. An advertisement for the essay appears at the back of his *A Soldier's Diary*: "A POT OF ROMAN GOLD—One of the most brilliant and lively essays ever written and on a strange theme, arising out of the discovery of a pot of Roman coins unearthed by an American soldier on a battlefield near Amiens. Price $1.50" (217).

The Battle of Amiens, August 8–11, 1918

After the success of the Soissons offensive, which ended August 2, it was the turn of the British to attack. The immediate objective was to free Amiens and the Amiens-Paris railroad from German artillery fire and to reduce the German salient, which was created during the first great German offensive of March 21.

By the end of the day on August 8, Australian, Canadian, and British troops, as part of Rawlinson's Fourth Army, had advanced eight miles on a nine-mile front, captured four hundred big guns, and inflicted twenty-seven thousand casualties on the German army, at a cost of nine thousand Allied casualties.

After the stunning successes of August 8, which Ludendorff would refer to as the "black day of the German Army," subsequent attacks were less well coordinated, and Allied casualties began to mount (Toland, *No Man's Land*, 373). Finally, on the eleventh the offensive was shut down. But the damage to German strength and morale was lasting, and the stage was set for a series of Allied thrusts that would, within three months, bring the Germans to surrender.

The sole American unit to participate in the Battle of Amiens was the 131st Infantry Regiment of the 33rd Division, which was detached for this purpose to the British 58th Division in the reserve of the British III Corps. The otherwise rapid Allied advance of August 8 ran into one serious impediment: a bare seventy-five-foot-high ridge in an oxbow bend on the north bank of the Somme, near Chipilly, which was still in German hands. From this eminence, German machine gunners poured a devastating enfilade fire onto the flank of the Australian corps across the river at Hamel. The job of clearing this ridge was given to the American 131st Regiment. Far from being in position to launch the attack at the designated zero hour of dawn on the ninth, the 131st was dispersed over a wide area, with the 1st and 2nd Battalions spread throughout an area of trenches northwest of Heilly, and the 3rd Battalion at Pierrogot, some twenty miles to the northwest. Throughout the day and night of the eighth and most of the ninth, the three units struggled to cover the distance, locate one another, and get into position at the jumping-off line.

For the men of the 131st, the night of August 8–9 was one of danger, fatigue, and utter disorientation. They had no information as to the nature of the terrain, and during the night of August 8–9, the 1st and 2nd Battalions were subject to both gas and artillery fire and able to locate one another only with the greatest difficulty. The 2nd Battalion marched without transports or Lewis machine guns and with one hundred pieces of small-arms ammunition per man; the 3rd Battalion had to cover the greatest distance without rations or water. After their night-long march, the men of the 3rd Battalion were forced to cover the final four miles at a run while carrying full packs.

Their attack took place at 5:30 P.M., and despite the heavy machine-gun and artillery fire pouring down on them from on Chipilly Ridge, the Americans could not be driven back. They repeatedly pressed the assault until the northern half of Chipilly Ridge and the southern end of nearby Gressair Wood were taken. Continuing the assault the following day, they took the remainder of Gressair Wood and by day's end were in possession of seven hundred German prisoners, thirty artillery pieces, one aircraft, and more than one hundred machine guns. A corporal of the 131st received the Medal of Honor for single-handedly capturing a machine-gun nest, killing five of the enemy, and taking fifteen prisoners.

Molliens-au-Bois: Division Headquarters

Probably August 8. This sonnet falls sometime between the Elsie Janis performance on July 19 and the Battle of Chipilly Ridge on August 9. During this period only one movement of an entire brigade took place, that of the 65th Brigade on August 6, but while it passed within sight of Wyeth's position, it did so at night; and it was not going to the front, only to another reserve position. During the period all large troop movements within sight of division headquarters took place in the evening or night, and mostly in rainy weather.

One possible exception is the movement of the 3rd Battalion, 131st Infantry. Following emergency orders to make their way to the front with all due haste and coming from the village of Pierrogot, they would have passed right through the headquarters camp, where Wyeth was located. The weather was clear on that day, and the roads were described as "good," meaning dry. Wyeth's sonnet depicts the troops marching at midday, but the 3rd Battalion was ordered to set out at 4:30 P.M. However, a preliminary order to make preparations for a move came down at 12:10, so, knowing how much ground they had to cover and how congested their single road would be, it may be that some elements of the battalion set out at once.

Aside from the question of literal accuracy, the martial image of troops marching to the front, with bayonets flashing in the sun, sets the stage for the sequence of six linked "Chipilly Ridge" sonnets that follow. The soldiers discuss the momentous and the mundane, and the issue of men marching toward death is eclipsed by the availability of chocolate at the YMCA. The Y found that chocolate ranked second only to tobacco as the item most requested by soldiers in the AEF.

The Six Chipilly Ridge Sonnets: The Night of August 8–9, 1918

See "The Battle of Amiens" (xxxix).

About fifteen miles east of Amiens, the Somme River makes a series of pronounced oxbow bends. Having first driven some twenty-five kilometers from Molliens-au-Bois, Wyeth and his companion pursue their course along the north bank of this stretch of the Somme from Corbie to Vaux-sur-Somme to Sailly-le-Sec to Sailly-Laurette. They travel first in an open staff car and then on foot throughout the dangerous, chaotic night of August 8–9. Wyeth does not identify the purpose of their nightlong journey.

The Road to Corbie

Late afternoon to early evening, August 8. By the time they set out late in the day in a staff car, Wyeth and his companion find the roads choked with trucks and columns of marching, pack-laden troops.

This is the 3rd Battalion of the 131st Infantry (see "The Battle of Amiens" [xxxix]), which may also have been depicted in the previous sonnet, "Division Headquarters." But if the identity of the marching troops is uncertain in the previous sonnet, their identity in this sonnet is clear, since only the 3rd Battalion of the 131st Infantry was on the road from Molliens-au-Bois to the front on August 8. Both battalion and staff car are bound for the north bank of the Somme, where the rest of the 131st is scheduled to rendezvous. The destination specified in the original orders was the village of Heilly, where headquarters of the British 58th Division is located; but by 10 P.M. the 131st has been ordered to an assembly point on the Bray-Corbie road, some three thousand yards to the south of Heilly, in readiness to attack an hour after midnight. Subsequently, however, because the men of the 1st and 2nd Battalions are exhausted, the terrain unreconnoitered, the troops without supplies, and the 3rd Battalion still in transit, the commanding general of the 58th decides to postpone the attack until evening of the ninth. The 131st is sent onward to the north bank of the Somme east of Corbie to a "position in readiness" in the valleys between Vaux-sur-Somme and Sailly-le-Sec. Corbie, the ruined village through which Wyeth and his companion pass, is located some fifteen kilometers east of Amiens, on the north bank of the Somme, at the confluence of the Somme and the Ancre (Huidekoper, *History of the 33rd Division*, 1:45).

Corbie to Sailly-le-Sec

Dusk, August 8. The distance from Corbie, eastward along the north bank of the Somme, following a large north-curving arc of the river and passing through Vaux-sur-Somme to the village of Sailly-le-Sec, is about five kilometers.

Chipilly Ridge: Regimental Headquarters

After nightfall, August 8. The headquarters of the 131st Regiment is located in a small wood about a thousand yards northwest of Sailly-le-Sec. From here, guided by runners, they will set out to locate 2nd Battalion headquarters.

Chipilly Ridge: Through the Valley

The night of August 8–9. Gas masks on and led by runners, Wyeth and Tom [Lieutenant Thomas J. Cochrane] set out on foot in search of 2nd Battalion headquarters, situated roughly six hundred yards to the south, close to the river. It becomes clear that the valley of the sonnet's title is the biblical Valley of Death.

Chipilly Ridge: Second Battalion Headquarters

The late hours of the night of August 8–9. Wyeth and Tom have reached 2nd Battalion headquarters, roughly eight hundred yards west and a little north of Sailly-le-Sec and some six or seven hundred yards north of the river Somme.

Chipilly Ridge: Regimental Dressing Station

Dawn, August 9. Exact location unknown, but somewhere in the vicinity of Sailly-Laurette, a kilometer or two to the east of Sailly-le-Sec, also on the Somme. In this makeshift dressing station full of wounded and dying men, Wyeth and Tom find themselves on the very edge of the combat zone, within three or four kilometers of where the Australians are pinned down by German machine-gun and artillery fire from Chipilly Ridge.

Molliens-au-Bois: British Concert Party

August 12. The occasion for this "concert party" is an 11 A.M. visit to 33rd Division headquarters at the Chateau of Molliens-au-Bois by King George V, accompanied by an impressive part of the British and American top brass, including General John J. Pershing, commander-in-chief of the American Expeditionary Force; General Tasker H. Bliss; and General Sir Henry Rawlinson, commander of the Fourth British Army.

Some three hundred men, selected from every unit of the division, are drawn up in formation on the chateau grounds as the king decorates twelve officers and enlisted men of the 33rd Division for gallantry at Hamel on July 4. Seven other men who are to be decorated cannot be present because they are hospitalized for wounds. After about half an hour the ceremony concludes, and the king departs.

In the evening the men of the division are entertained on the chateau grounds by an English troupe, the Follies, who are depicted in Wyeth's sonnet. They sing a wide range of songs, give readings, dance, and perform short dramatic sketches. The final image of the mournful clown singing "Roses are shining in Picardy" is particularly poignant; all the fatalities of the division have occurred in Picardy.

The songs referred to are "Yaaka Hula Hickey Dula" (1916), words and music by E. Ray Goetz, Joe Young, and Pete Wendling; "For Me and My Gal" (1917), words by Edgar Leslie and E. Ray Goetz, music by George W. Meyer; and "Roses of Picardy" (1916), words by Fred E. Weatherly, music by Haydn Wood.

Three Sonnets: A Drive by Motorcycle to the Australian Front to Deliver Maps to the 132nd Regiment, August 15, 1918
On August 8, as Wyeth and the 131st Regiment were making their way to the Somme—the day before the assault on Chipilly Ridge—three Australian and one Canadian division, as part of the same Amiens counteroffensive by the Fourth British Army to which the 131st was attached, were launching attacks against German positions just to the south of the Somme. Bayonvillers, about eight kilometers south of Chipilly, was taken by the Australian 5th Division, while Harbonnières, about three and one half kilometers to the southeast of Bayonvillers, was taken by the Australian 2nd Division. Wyeth, riding in a motorcycle sidecar, is in search of an American regiment billeted somewhere among the Australians. This is the 132nd Regiment, 33rd Division, which has just moved from Querrieu Wood (where they were in reserve) by trucks to Bayonvillers on August 15 under orders from the Australian 4th Division.

———

The Road to Bayonvillers

August 15. The distance between Molliens-au-Bois and Bayonvillers is roughly twenty-eight kilometers. Bois Vert, evidently a small wood somewhere between Amiens and Bayonvillers, does not appear on the map of operations, the map of the Somme offensive, or the situation map of August 8. Bayonvillers, the scene of at least one battle between a Canadian tank and a German artillery crew on August 8, now lies in ruins, reeking from bodies that have lain unburied in the late summer heat for the past week.

Harbonnières: Regimental Maps from Headquarters

Sunset, August 15. No one seems to know the location of the 132nd because it has only just arrived in the area this morning. Wyeth locates it in the vicinity of Harbonnières, three or four kilometers southeast of Bayonvillers, and turns over the maps he is carrying to the commanding officer, Colonel Abel Davis. The regiment is on the verge of leaving for the front line, where it will relieve the Australian 12th Brigade, 4th Division, and there is no time to have the maps distributed among Davis's companies. Wyeth's two-day, sixty-kilometer mission from and now back to Molliens-au-Bois has been for naught.

Harbonnières to Bayonvillers: Picnic

Morning, August 16. The German signs are marks of the occupation that had come to an end only one week before.

Molliens-au-Bois: Headquarters Troop Kitchen

Sometime between August 17–20.

For more information on the headquarters troop, see "First Lieutenant Wyeth and 33rd Division Headquarters Troop" (xlix).

33rd Division Transferred from British to American Command; Molliens-au-Bois to Tronville-en-Barrois, August 23–25, 1918

In late August 1918 the entire 33rd Division was transferred from the British army in the Amiens sector to the First American Army in the Toul sector. It traveled by train, leaving on the morning of August 23 from three different stations: Vignacourt, St. Roch, and Longueau. Wyeth, as part of division headquarters, leaves from Vignacourt at 8:11 A.M. The new division headquarters are opened in the chateau at Tronville-en-Barrois, about eleven kilometers southeast of Bar-le-Duc. The distance of the two-day journey is approximately 325 kilometers.

This is the first journey made by Wyeth while in France that he does not depict in his sonnet sequence.

————

Tronville-en-Barrois: Night Watch

Sometime between August 25 and September 5. During the ten days that the division is at Tronville, it undergoes a period of training, as part of the First American Army, including a divisional terrain exercise on September 3. This sonnet is the only one set during the three-and-one-half weeks from August 16 to September 8.

The lyrics are from "I Ain't Got Nobody Much and Nobody Cares for Me" ("I Ain't Got Nobody"; 1916), with music by Spencer Williams, words by Roger Graham.

Blercourt: La Voie Sacrée

September 8 or 9. On September 5, 1918, orders are received from the First American Army placing the 33rd Division "at the disposal" of the XVII Corps of the Second French Army and directing it to proceed to the Blercourt area.

La Voie Sacrée, "The Sacred Way" (over which Wyeth has just traveled on his way to Blercourt), refers to the sixty-kilometer stretch of narrow, crushed-stone road that, in early 1916, became the main artery between Bar-le-Duc and Verdun, at a time when the German army was determined to obliterate Verdun and destroy France and almost succeeded. This road, over which tens of thousands of army supply vehicles crawled bumper-to-bumper, day and night, for ten straight months, enabled the defense of Verdun to continue until December 1916, when the Germans finally called off their siege. A third of a million French soldiers died at Verdun.

Fromeréville: In a Dugout

Between September 11 and September 13. No sooner are 33rd Division headquarters opened at Blercourt on September 7 than new orders come down that evening from the French XVII Corps for relief of elements of the French 157th and 120th Divisions in the line near Cumières and Mort Homme. The relief takes place on the nights of September 7, 8, and 9, with command passing to the 33rd Division at 8:00 A.M., September 10. That same morning division headquarters, including Wyeth, moves some twelve kilometers closer to the front to the small village of Fromeréville—a move intended to divert German attention from the actual attack at St. Mihiel.

Fromeréville: Party

Dusk, sometime between September 11–13. The "Troop" is headquarters troop, a small cavalry/liaison/security unit of about 125 enlisted men and 3 officers attached to division headquarters (see "Lempire: Headquarters Troop Barracks" [li]). The "ashes to ashes" couplet was attached to various blues songs.

Battle of St. Mihiel, September 12–16, 1918

On September 12, in the first major American action of the war under American command, ten divisions (216,000 men) of the First American Army under General Pershing, supported by four French divisions (48,000 men), launched an attack on the St. Mihiel salient against 75,000 German troops under General von Fuchs. The Allies advanced five miles along a twelve-mile front in heavy rain, and by the sixteenth had taken 15,000 German prisoners of war and 450 guns at a cost of 7,511 American and 597 French casualties.

The infantry regiments of the 33rd Division did not participate directly in this offensive, but the 52nd Artillery Brigade of the division took part in diversionary firing from the Bois de Sartelles, just south of Fromeréville, designed to divert German attention from the actual attack at St. Mihiel.

Fromeréville: War in Heaven

The afternoon of September 14. According to the records of the German air service, the German pilot was almost certainly Unteroffizier Hans Heinrich Marwede of Jagdstaffel 67, who was credited on this date with shooting down three balloons in five minutes, at about 4:35 in the afternoon, southwest of Verdun.

Build-up for the Impending Meuse-Argonne Offensive, in the Days Prior to September 26, 1918

From about September 15 on, the men of the 33rd Division who were billeted in Fromeréville, including Lieutenant Wyeth, were subject to recurrent artillery fire and aerial bombardment. Because Fromeréville was a bottleneck on the route to the front, a continuous stream of heavy traffic—supply trucks, artillery, staff vehicles, officers on reconnaissance, and troops of every sort—passed through from dusk until dawn.

On September 14, the 33rd Division passed under the control of the American III Corps. During the final week before the offensive, there was some shifting of units within the division and a bolstering of the front trenches by additional companies of the 132nd before settling on a configuration that satisfied corps headquarters. On September 22 the American III Corps, including the 33rd Division, passed to the control of the First American Army.

On September 25 the command posts of 33rd Division headquarters and the 52nd Field Artillery Brigade were moved from Fromeréville to "P.C. la Hutte," a dugout in the Bois Burrus about one and one-half kilometers to the north, in readiness for the attack of the following morning.

Wyeth did not accompany division headquarters to the Bois Burrus, but instead moved with headquarters troop to Lempire, eight kilometers southwest of Verdun and six and one-half kilometers west of the Meuse.

Fort de Landrecourt: Above Verdun

Between September 27 and October 19. Fort de Landrecourt was one of thirty-six forts situated on the hills around Verdun, a legacy of the Franco-Prussian War when the Germans located their batteries on these same hills to shell the city. One of the five larger forts forming the west front of fortifications, it was located about five kilometers west of the Meuse and six kilometers southwest of Verdun. From Wyeth's billet in Lempire, the fort was two and one-half kilometers to the northwest.

Wyeth approaches the fort on horseback and reads the legend above the gate: BURY ONESELF BENEATH THE RUINS OF THE FORT RATHER THAN SURRENDER. He is stopped by a French sentry, with whom he has a cordial exchange. Wyeth inquires, "One cannot visit?" to which the sentry replies, "Without permission? Sorry about that." As Wyeth rides away, he looks down on the ruins of Verdun, which he hears cry out, "Let the dead rise!"

Lempire: Entente Cordiale

Between September 27 and October 19. "Entente Cordial" means, literally, "friendly agreement." The term had been in use since 1844 to acknowledge the existence of common interests between France and Britain. Later it was used in reference to the 1904 agreement between the two nations. During the First World War, the phrases *the Entente, the Triple Entente, the Entente Powers,* and *the Entente Forces* all referred to the allied nations united in their opposition to Germany.

In this sonnet an entente cordial takes place between a French waiter and three Americans in a Lempire café. The waiter comments on a colored postcard featuring an eagle and a rooster, national symbols of America and France.

First Lieutenant Wyeth and 33rd Division Headquarters Troop

The divisional unit mentioned most frequently in *This Man's Army* is the headquarters troop, a small cavalry/liaison/security unit attached to the division headquarters. At least two of the officers of 33rd Division Headquarters Troop appear in Wyeth's sonnets: the commander of the troop, Captain Herbert W. Styles, and Wyeth's frequent companion "Tommy," First Lieutenant Thomas J. Cochrane.

The headquarters troop was a vestige of the prewar cavalry regiment, and indeed, all three officers of 33rd Division Headquarters Troop were cavalry officers. Originally there had been one cavalry regiment per division but, with the prospect of entering the European war with its ubiquitous trenches, static lines, and fortified positions, the cavalry regiment in American army divisions, under advice of European military planners, was eliminated except for a remnant of about 150 men and 3 officers. On paper a headquarters troop was to be fully equipped with mounts, as well as a sizable number of motorcycles and cars, but how they were equipped in practice has not been recorded.

Just how Wyeth was associated with 33rd Division Headquarters Troop is uncertain. He was not officially assigned to the headquarters troop, as by prescription such a troop was to have only one captain and two lieutenants, and it already had them without Wyeth; nor is he included in their officers' roster. Yet Wyeth does appear to have been attached to the headquarters troop.

Then just prior to the Argonne offensive, when division headquarters and headquarters troop are moved in opposite directions— division headquarters going forward toward the front, while headquarters troop moves back to the village of Lempire—Wyeth, rather than going forward with headquarters, moves back to Lempire with the troop.

The precise function of the headquarters troop in the American army during World War I is unclear. It appears that not every division in the AEF had a headquarters troop and that there was considerable variation in how the troop, in each case, was employed. It was recommended that troop functions include liaison (delivering messages from division headquarters to subordinate units throughout the division) and work details, which could include any sort of manual labor. One source indicates that in the AEF the headquarters troop functioned as a kind of catchall for officers of the general staff (such as translators) who were not part of the commanding officer's immediate staff. Other sources suggest that the headquarters troop was frequently employed in guard duty and other security functions, including cooperative assignments with the military police.

When Wyeth describes his own duties, they seem to fit this same description. He delivers messages and maps to the front line (by car, motorcycle, and on foot).

Sources: I am indebted to Pat Holscher, Neal O'Brien, Niall Ferguson, Jim Broshot, Len Shurtleff, Nicker Forder, "Dreadnought," Gary Reavell, Philip Sauerlender, and members of the World War I Military History Discussion Group (Kansas State University), the forum of the Society of the Military Horse, the Great War Forum, and the Lost Generation 14–18 Forum for their expert and detailed discussion regarding the nature and function of the headquarters troop in AEF divisions.

————

Lempire: Headquarters Troop Barracks

The calls in the craps game are contradictory: "box cars" and "snake eyes" are losing throws.

Lempire: Souvenirs

Between September 27 and October 19. There were no sixteen-year-old pilots in the German air service; the youngest were eighteen.

Souilly: Hospital

In October, before the nineteenth. Wyeth is in an evacuation hospital in Souilly. The subsequent sonnet reveals that he has influenza.

Instructions for evacuation issued by headquarters, 33rd Division, in late September specified that the serious noncontagious sick, the wounded, and those patients requiring operations were to be evacuated to Evacuation Hospitals No. 6 or 7 at Souilly. It is to one of these two evacuation hospitals that Wyeth has been taken.

Source: I am particularly grateful to Alan Albright, historian for the American Field Service (see http://www.ourstory.info/), for information on the role of Souilly in the First World War and on French hospitals of evacuation.

Hospital Train

Sometime in October. Wyeth is on a Red Cross hospital train, somewhere along the 550-kilometer rail journey from Souilly to Angers. He is being sent back to Base Hospital 27 in Angers, which, according to every soldier who passes through there, is "the paradise of the wounded man" (Stallings, *The Doughboys,* 185). Base Hospital 27 was renowned for the expert ministrations of its nursing staff, most of whom came from Mercy Hospital in Pittsburgh, Pennsylvania.

By the end of the campaign Americans had suffered some 117,000 casualties, with 4,000 of those coming from the ranks of the 33rd Division. Influenza was frequently deadly. By October 1918 some 20,000 American soldiers had died from the combination of flu and pneumonia. It came to be generally believed that this influenza—which would kill 40 million people worldwide—was a direct result of the war itself.

Sources

Abbott, Lynn, and Doug Seroff. "'They Cert'ly Sound Good to Me': Sheet Music, Southern Vaudeville, and the Commercial Ascendancy of the Blues." *American Music* 14 (Winter 1996): 402–54.

American Battle Monuments Commission. *American Armies and Battlefields in Europe: A History, Guide, and Reference Book*. Washington, D.C.: U.S. Government Printing Office, 1938.

American Battle Monuments Commission. *33rd Division, Summary of Operations in the World War*. Washington, D.C.: U.S. Government Printing Office, 1944.

Coffman, Edward M. *The War to End All Wars*. New York: Oxford University Press, 1968.

Collins, V. Lansing. *Princeton in the World War*. Princeton, N.J.: Office of the Secretary, Princeton University, 1932.

Franks, Norman L. R., Frank W. Bailey, and Rick Duiven. *Casualties of the German Air Service, 1914–1920: As Complete a List Possible Arranged Chronologically and Alphabetically*. London: Grub Street, 1999.

Gray, Randal. *Chronicle of the First World War*. With Christopher Argyle. 2 vols. New York: Facts on File, 1991.

Haller, John S., Jr. *Farmcarts to Fords: A History of the Military Ambulance, 1790–1925*. Carbondale: Southern Illinois University Press, 1992.

Handy, W. C. *Father of the Blues*. New York: Macmillan, 1941.

Huidekoper, Frederic Louis. *The History of the 33rd Division, A.E.F.* 4 vols. Springfield: Illinois State Historical Library, 1921.

Janis, Elsie. *The Big Show: My Six Months with the American Expeditionary Forces*. New York: Cosmopolitan, 1919.

Judy, Captain Will. *A Soldier's Diary: A Day-to-Day Record in the World War*. Chicago: Judy Publishing Company, 1930.

Keegan, John. *An Illustrated History of the First World War*. New York: A. A. Knopf, 2001.

Lighter, Jonathan. "The Slang of the American Expeditionary Forces in Europe, 1917–1919: An Historical Glossary," *American Speech* 47 (Spring–Summer 1972): 5–142.

Maurois, André. *I Remember, I Remember*. Translated by Denver and Jane Lindley. New York: Harper, 1942.

Service with Fighting Men: An Account of the Work of the American Young Men's Christian Associations in the World War. 2 vols. New York: Association Press, 1922.

Stallings, Laurence. *The Doughboys: The Story of the AEF, 1917–1918.* New York: Harper & Row, 1963.

Thomas, Shipley. *The History of the A.E.F.* New York: Doran, 1920.

Toland, John. *No Man's Land: 1918, the Last Year of the Great War.* Garden City, N.Y.: Doubleday, 1980.

Wilgus, William J. *Transporting the A.E.F. in Western Europe.* New York: Columbia University Press, 1931.

This Man's Army

TO MY MOTHER

CAMP UPTON

SAILING ORDERS

Raw barracks blistering in a waste of sand
and scrubby oak and scrawny stunted pine—
Not much to show you in this desolate place,
a desert, even in the month of May.
It seems more real to sit here hand in hand
indoors, at tea, and know that you are mine,
all of you mine for just a little space.
Tea comes and goes and with it our last day . . .
All this you cannot fail to understand—
our final silence is a mutual sign
unbroken by the station shouts and cries,
our almost happy casual embrace,
your strange "A . . . dieu," and as you go away
my dreary smile and your appalling eyes.

CAMP UPTON TO HOBOKEN

SECRET TROOP MOVEMENT

A night march under black skies faintly starred—
the trudging columns tramp and jostle by.
"Cut out that smokin', goddamm it, do as you're told—
No talking there—we don't want any noise."
A scrunch of gravel in the station yard.
We ride all night—The men curl up and lie
askew on the seats and stretch against the cold.
All out by dawn—the harbor pale turquoise
with tugboats belching dirty smoke from charred
smokestacks. We ferry to Hoboken. Clear and high,
with sunrise cutting every roof and quoin,
a skyline all grey shadow slit with gold.
A downtown ferry passes—
                              "Give 'em hell, boys."
"Giv'em hell yourself, it's not too late to join."

THE TRANSPORT

I

A thick still heat stifles the dim saloon.
The rotten air hangs heavy on us all,
and trails a steady penetrating steam
of hot wet flannel and the evening's mess.
Close bodies swaying, catcalls out of tune,
while the jazz band syncopates the *Darktown Strutters' Ball*,
we crowd like minnows in a muddy stream.
O God, even here a sense of loneliness . . .
I grope my way on deck to watch the moon
gleam sharply where the shadows rise and fall
in the immense disturbance of the sea.
And like the vast possession of a dream
that black ship, and the pale sky's emptiness,
and this great wind become a part of me.

THE TRANSPORT

II

I know the coast of Brittany will rise
for me tomorrow with the break of day—
but this dark windy hour is full of fear.
A subtle panic leaves the night aghast.
Death must be passing somewhere, and my eyes
stare at the stars fixed in their bleak dismay,
search all along the fumbling clouds, and peer
through the black cordage of the dizzy mast
into the haunted moon. And all this lies
beyond me, where the grim destroyers play.
Here is a thing in which I have no part—
it drives me down, below, where men are near.
I stumble on them—fiercely glad, at last,
to hear "For Christ's sake Buddy have a heart!"

BREST

THE WATERWAY

The sky all blue and clear and high with noon
above the green and grey profile of Brest.
France!—and my heart like a flag in a slapping wind,
straining and gay—and secretive with joy.
A plane over the bay and a green balloon.
From every rail and rigging and crow's-nest
men waving, and their cheering swelled and thinned
to silence as we passed their long convoy.
Stillness.   How quiet green trees are—and soon
the massive feel of a great ship at rest.
A little Breton boat put out to sea
and brown old fishwives waved at us and grinned.
"Yea—"
       "*Hey* there—"
                "*O* Boy *look* at 'em wave—"
                                "Atta*boy*."
'*It's the* wild *wild* women'—
                "Yea—"
                    '*They're* ma*kin*' *a* wild *man o*' me.'

BREST

THE WATERFRONT

Down there, below this plunge of granite wall,
trucks jolt across an empty trolley track.
Dockyards and secret barrels—on the piers
men lounging against crates and bales of hay.
A slender jetty—painted troopships all
a blaze of jagged stripes. A fishing smack
with a slow sail like rusty velvet steers
across the satin shimmer of the bay.
The way these trees come down the sloping mall!
A woman sitting there, in shabby black,
lonely and dull— God is all France to be
like her, too casual and numb for tears,
and white loose hands forgotten in a way
to make my heart break almost out of me.

THE TRAIN FROM BREST

A haze of dusk behind low roofs of thatch
and sloping moors and barren gouty trees—
dim roads and earth-walled fields—the steady flight
of blinking poles and the rhythmic sweep of wires.
Darkness outside—
                    "Hey Tommy, gimme a match—
now gimme a Lucky."
                    "You're sorta hard to please—
you don't want much."
                    —"Somebody turn off the light
I want to sleep."
                    "Hell—with these frog flat tires?"
A stifling blackness—sweat, and the jiggling scratch
of cloth on your neck and tickling under the knees,
and the clank of iron beating a rackety tune—
and like a secret calling in the night
waking to see the black cathedral spires
of Chartres against a low-hung lazy moon.

ON TO PARIS

Light enough now to watch the trees go by—
a sleep like sickness in the rattling train.
Men's bodies joggle on the opposite seat
and tired greasy faces half awake
stir restlessly and breathe a stagnant sigh.
The stale air thickens on the grimy pane
reeking of musty smoke and woolly feet.
Versailles—a bridge of shadow on a lake
dawn-blue and pale, the color of the sky.
Paris at last!—and a great joy like pain
in my heart. We scuffle down the corridor.
"Lieutenant."
                "Sir."
                        "In half an hour we meet
at another station—your orders are to take
these men by subway to the Gare du Nord."

THE BRITISH FRONT

Noon on the white cathedral of Beauvais,
a glaring brittle hull of stone and glass
long after glittering above the plain.
A halt at a junction—
                    "Get back—*Stay* where you are!"
"All out!"
          "My God I'm *shaving*—"
                              "Get out of the way—"
"Jump *damn* you—"
              "Throw the bags out—"
                              A breathless mass
crushing and scrambling in the moving train,
and men and packs plunge out of every car.
Another train, through slow green hills all day—
American troops that wave and shout as we pass
"What outfit—*Hey*—"
                    Long salvage trains.   We shunt
along and stall.   And like a pumping vein,
our eardrums jump and catch from very far
the muffled pulse of guns along the front.

OISEMONT

PLACE DE LA MAIRIE

The shadows slant along the dusty square
that tilts haphazard past the blank Mairie.
Grey timid little houses hand in hand
step gingerly downhill. A yellow wall,
branded *Hôtel du Soleil d'Or*—down there
the zinc and tinware sign *Quincaillerie*.
Up from the rest camp swings a Highland band
and people swarm and clutter . . . children call.
The pipers drone a shrill nostalgic air
below my window in the Mercerie,
kilts flapping while the drumsticks thump and fly.
The gaunt old belfry tolls a reprimand,
and as the drums stop and the bagpipes squall
a long slow dingy funeral crawls by.

OISEMONT

BRITISH DETRAINING STATION

All night the lumbering troop trains jolted in
and choked the yard with soldiers all night long
who swore and chuckled, yawned and scrunched away . . .
Silence . . . A half-sleep numbs and tickles me.
The grey dawn shivers on my grimy skin.
Cognac, and coffee villainously strong,
—and no trains due to spoil my holiday!
"Oh righto Texas, don't be late for tea."
Already morning, and the market's din.
Across the steep square with its shabby throng
I stroll downhill to lie in the grass and feel
how wide the hot earth is in June—and play
with sleep, and wake up just enough to see
those frail trees and the town's naïve profile.

HUPPY

HUPPY

So many shadows that the air is green . . .
Light catches in the upper leaves and dies
along the slim white belfry by the park.
Ducks waddle home, self-conscious on the ground.
Some trim young Red Tabs in a limousine
scatter a drifting dust cloud in our eyes.
A soldier blithely whistles *Joan of Arc.*
Gates shut and jangle . . . Bugles thinly sound . . .
Twilight, and after mess a round of *'fine.'*
They're bombing Abbeville! Lights crack, searchlights rise—
a woman runs and screams "Jules—Jean—où êtes-*vous?*"
They fill the road . . . one hails me in the dark,
her five grandchildren pressing close around—
"Qu'allons-nous faire?—Nous avons peur chez nous!"

HUPPY

THE LIFE O' RILEY

"Come on, we're goin' down to the old café."

"It's closed after nine—we'll land in the calaboose
if the M. P.'s get us."

           "Hell, we'll slip out the back
through a window—"

           "All right—don't raise a hell of a row."

—"Bonsoir, Messieurs—tout est fermé."

           "Allez
toot sweet to hell, une bouteille de *Banyuls.*"

"Alors pas de bruit, Messieurs."

           "Bring us some Black
and White *whiskey.*"

           "Voilà Messieurs."

           "That's the stuff—Here's how."

"Hey Mademeselle—*Ici*—S'il vous plait
fenetre—police—*ouvrir* . . . Aw what's the use."

—"Well Skipper, brandy or rum?"

           "I don't care which—
tell her to step on it."

           "Tout le monde *cognac*
toot sweet—O Boy You're *in* the army now—"

'You're not *behind the* plow—*You'll* never *get* rich'—

EU

The sunlight quivers in the gusty air
that blows like music through the hot June day.
Salt sea winds heavy with the smell of land—
a drift of blue-white clouds across pure sky.
High-shouldered roofs beyond the sandy square
and smutty chimneys breathing all one way.
Two clipped green rows of dusty lindens stand
around that old house and the canvas Y.
Close-shuttered, barred, and blindly unaware
of the empty circus tent Y M C A,
it squatters there, more evil than before,
like some foul prison on the hard-baked sand,
antique and bawdy, with a queue of shy
and ribald soldiers standing at the door.

EU

INTERIOR

"Descendez toutes, là-haut—descendez vite!
Ce sont des clients—mais dépêches-toi ma chère."
Into the sordid room the girls defile
like dreary mimes, unhappy and impure.
"Champagne Madame—Some *du* vin."
     "Oui, tout d'suite
Messieurs."
  "Toot sweet is right."
    —"Allons donc, c'est la guerre,
soyez plus gaies!"
   The sallow faces smile.
"Say look at the one with the yellow curls."
      "She sure
is a Lulu, I'll tell the world."
    —"Allez mes petites,
chantez-leur la chanson de la *Porte-Cochère.*"
—"Encore champagne! Here, fill 'em up you guys."
—"Allô, chéri"—a low voice sleek with guile—
here come her thin arms and the ancient lure
of pathos in her unfamiliar eyes.

LE TRÉPORT

THE SEASHORE

Letters from home—and this first one from you
which I have kept with me all day unread
and now and then forgotten, called to mind,
and here brought with me, down to the edge of the sea.
A fragile new moon glitters where the blue
thins into gold beyond a sea of lead,
and little waves break down and leave behind
a sift of singing foam unceasingly.
Still light enough to read—and as I do,
the rhythmic cliffs go pale, and overhead
stars come and tremble, delicate and green.
And something in my heart leaps high to find
that you are somehow all the more with me
because of this great reach of sea between.

EU TO MOLLIENS-AU-BOIS

MOTOR CONVOY

A café on the Place Sadi Carnot,
and crowded trucks lined up along the square.
"Vite, déjeuner, Madame—une ommelette
avec douze oeufs, compree?"
                              And halfway through,
"They're cranking up!"
                "Combien, *quick*—"
                              "Run, there they go!"
Then all day riding in the stifling glare
jigging and rattling, faces caked with sweat
and white dust.
                "Want a swig?"
                              "I'll say I do."
Southward the towers of Amiens prick the low
straight edge of sky, and in the heat-blue air
long green fields melt in the hazy plain.   Our trucks
pull up at Molliens-au-Bois—a steep road set
with mud-walled barns and brick farms, and a few
dry willows by a brown pond streaked with ducks.

MOLLIENS-AU-BOIS

The sunset sharpens all those distant hills,
and shadows meet and lose themselves below.
A wash of violet slowly deepens where
the colors of the valley die away.
A hidden chimney lazily distils
a breath of smoke into the afterglow.
The long grey roads are empty—over there
a lonely peasant dimly stacking hay.
The moon begins between two drowsy mills,
and evening gathers back of the chateau,
where dusk and darkness subtly interfuse—
—And all this vibrant with the maddest air
from that wood blaring like a cabaret
the brazen clamor of the *Beale Street Blues*.

MOLLIENS-AU-BOIS

REGIMENTAL CONCERT

A late green afternoon—the chateau grounds
covered with figures sprawling in the damp
cool grass, around the band.
                    "Who's that frog there?"
"The Duke of Mulliens."
                    "Shut up, there's singing!"
                                        . . . *'Just*
a Baby's Prayer at Twilight' . . . ends in rounds
of applause.
            —"Here comes the Aussies up from the camp—
they're wild men."
                —"Look at the Duke's horse! He don't care
for the *Livery Stable Blues,* say not for dust."
"D'you blame the animal the way it sounds?"
—"Is that the fellow who sings, with the beard and the tramp
overalls? He looks like a regular hayseed from Maine."
"Watch this, I seen him do this before—he's a bear
at spitting, all right."
                —*'Well, I swan, I must*
b'gettin on, (fft) *Giddap, Napoleon, it looks like rain'*—

MOLLIENS-AU-BOIS

ALLIES

"What the hell's going on in your tent?"

"Come on inside,
we're swinging a party in here. I want you to meet
the new British major—he's been detailed over here
to help us look after our horses—*Major.*"

"Wot—o!"

"Shake hands with my bunkie—when he ain't cockeyed
he's a damn good egg."

"Hy fellows."

"We got a treat
for you—just try this swell new liqueur called *Byrrh.*"

"My God that's a *tonic*—gimme some Scotch."

"Cheery-o
you bloody young Indians—Wot's the book he's tryin' to hide?
By Jove it's old Virgil—I wager I can repeat
all of Book IV—I haven't seen it in years.
You're not such damned savages!"

—"Pass the liquor, old dear."

"Here's how, Major—Give us a song."

"Right-o
my lads—'O *Mademeselle from Armenteers*'—"

MOLLIENS-AU-BOIS

AIR RAID

Reading, at night, the shutters closed and barred,
a candle by my mattress on the floor,
my Virgil open to the mellow flame,
I heard what seemed a racking change of gear—
like some truck mired outside the stable yard . . .
The stricken pages shook—A vast smash tore
at the room, and through the blackness came
a bestial angry grinding drone, and fear.
Arms crossed, fists clenched against my throat gone hard,
my body straining at the engine's roar,
at every blast a thing like joy . . . and soon
a lifted spell, and life somehow the same,
dragging me out to join the others near
the pond—a mud pit gaping at the moon!

MOLLIENS-AU-BOIS

GENERAL ORDER

"Cut out the singing, don't you know they're dead
men in the village? Blown to bits—the hicks
had lights in their tents."
                          "How many got it?"
                                          "Four."
—"You heard the new order?"
                          "One got done up brown,
stood up to drink—we couldn't find his head."
—"Say Headquarters is in a hell of a fix,
they can't find men enough to dig the floor
of the officers' tents—they got to be dug down
three feet by sundown—Bet they're seeing red!"

—"Hello you staff birds, get to work—'BY SIX
THE FLOOR OF EVERY TENT MUST BE'—"
                                          "Go tell
the General where to get off."
                          "You make us sore,
just 'cause you got a cellar in the town—"
"You lousy shavetail, beat it, go to hell—"

MOLLIENS-AU-BOIS

THE VILLAGE ROAD

Too dark and late for any bugle call . . .
A wakeful horse along the picket line
stamps obstinately in the squashy loam.
No voice in either orchard with its dim
array of tents. Near by, a cracked old wall
gives, as I pass, a tiny blinking sign—
Bob must be still at work, or writing home.
I break in just to say goodnight to him . . .
Then half-way to my billet, being all
alone I bare my head before the shrine
that hallows all this stretch of road for me.
The sky-line flares and thunders, where a foam
of rockets drifts along the low charred rim
of hills that close in that infernal sea.

MOLLIENS-AU-BOIS

BRITISH SQUADRONS

An unlatched panel in my barnyard gate
opens clandestinely to let me in.
Some chickens stir and croon. The damp night air
is rankly tainted by a stable heap.
A light in Raichlin's window—not too late
to *'bavarder'* before the raids begin.
Our talk grows drowsy in the candle's flare
and all our silences are half asleep.
"Bonsoir."
         "Bonsoir, mon vieux."
                      We separate.
By now the sky is humming with a thin
strong drone of planes, and I undo the bars
of the heavy shutters, leaning out to stare
at that direct small light wherewith they keep
a straight course through a labyrinth of stars.

MOLLIENS-AU-BOIS

ALARUMS

A shutter rattles, and the garden door
jumps at the dull tumultuous cannonade.
My black room tingles with a long-drawn clear
sonorous flight of squadrons, faint and high.
Ah, there he comes . . . Thin streaks of light explore
the humming walls as searchlights pass and fade.
"Holà mon vieux," calls Raichlin—then I hear
his rapid knock, and an old woman's cry.
The Archies break out in a brute uproar.
We wait at the cellar stairs to judge the raid.
Frantic machine guns stutter, brusque shells blaze
in the light-swept clouds where, ominously near,
a beast wheels in the apocalyptic sky
and plunges through a stack of blinding rays.

MOLLIENS-AU-BOIS

ABRI

Oh Christ! why couldn't it have rained all night—
dizzy, half sick with sleep we stumble back
into our 'cave.'
   "On n'est pas mal ici,"
quavers Madame, "j'ai mis de la paille par terre."
Three chairs, one blanket, and a tiny light
in the fireplace, masked by a gunny sack.
They talk across my stupor.
     "Et Paris,
vous l'avez vu?"
    "Une fois, avant la guerre—"
The bombs come down the highway . . . Stiff with fright
I hear her beads click through the blind attack—
—"Les Parisiens ne pouvaient rien comprendre
de notre patois."
    Raichlin yawns. "C'est fini
Madame, montons, je crève."
      "Qu'allez-vous faire?
Y'a rien qui presse, on pourrait bien attendre."

MOLLIENS-AU-BOIS

HOME MAIL

"There's seven sacks of mail—nothing for you,
I asked 'em."
    "Will you look at what I got?"
"You dirty bum."
    "She says the baby's fine—"
"Say *Louis'* drafted!"
    "Aw he'll never go."

A blue green morning with a feel of dew
still in the air, and fields already hot,
and high-hung branches shifting a design
of faint grey leaves across the white chateau.

"Get anything?"
    "Yes, sir . . . oh, nothing new—
it's just the wife."
    "Here buck up, old man—What
is it?"
   "*Don't* tell anybody, I couldn't stand . . .
she says she's gone off with a friend of mine.
God damn her, look—Read that, sir."
       My dear Joe,
I'm crying as I take my pen in hand . . .

MOLLIENS-AU-BOIS

THE OLD ARMY GAME

"Hello . . . . . Yes, G-2's office . . . . . . No, he's not . . . .
He didn't say . . . . . . I'm sorry, I can't hear . . . .
You've got a *what* . . . a *bomb?* . . . From last night? . . . No,
just *leave* it there, we'll send someone around . . .
You think it's a new kind? . . . Yes, well thanks a lot . . .
No *no* don't send it anywhere, is that clear? . . .
Goodby, I'll tell him when he comes in . . . . . . Righto."

A hot green hour asleep with summer sound.

. . . "Oh hello—"
          "Here's the bomb, Lieutenant."
                              "*Where?*"
                                        "We got

it right here."
          "Don't come *in!* We don't want it anywhere *near.*
Bring it down to the Ordnance—it'll take ten years
off the Major's life! Don't *drop* the damn thing—go slow."

. . . "Sir."
          "Yes—My God, *get out!* Put it down on the ground—
God dammit sergeant call up the Engineers."

MOLLIENS-AU-BOIS

NEW DIGGINGS IN THE ORCHARD

Our two cots mudbound in a narrow pit,
a single candle's light shut in by tiers
of sandbags and a sheet iron tunnel vault.
"What's that you're reading?"
                    "*Through The Looking-Glass.*"
"It's late—Whose is it, yours?"
                    "I borrowed it
from the new captain in the Engineers."
"Read some out loud."
                    '*It was the black kitten's fault
entirely*' . . . so the tale runs and the chapters pass
and sleep begins.
                    . . . '*You wo'n't make yourself a bit
realler by crying. . . . And actually here's
a little brook! . . . He said 'You needn't shout
so loud!*'—'
                    "That's a German plane, Bob—let's call a halt,
he might lay an egg."
                    Then footsteps in the grass—
"Hey put your light out, down there—Jerry's out."

MOLLIENS-AU-BOIS

DIVISIONAL MANEUVERS

"How's the liaison, Major?"
                          "Not so warm—
The General's been ringin' me up all day—'G-2?
Hello!—*Well* Major, are you *functioning?*'
'Yes *sir*, I'm *func*tioning'—and here I set
all dolled up in my brand new uniform
and not *one* goddam message going through!"

Westward the hot sky curdles, thundering.
By the blazing roadside, men lie down and sweat.
"Fall in!"
              "Now where do we go—"
                                    Ahead of the storm
a rush of low loose clouds, flat-bellied, blue,
and a bleaching wind whips over the hissing plain.
A white split of fire, and thunder on thunder—the sting
of crepitant hail—and sweeping along, a wet
grey fringe of storm and the violent plunging of rain.

MOLLIENS-AU-BOIS

CONCERT BY ELSIE JANIS

Music and laughter in the late cool air
and thousands listening, close packed on the wet
green lawn, breathless like children in a trance.
"Yea *Elsie!*"
        "Move up, fellows, fill up the front pews—
'*Je ne* veux *pas guerir, car j'adore ma jolee infirmière . . .*'
'*Gif me the moonlight, gif me some bombs . . .*'
                    Here's my pet
darky story—Two niggers in jail, somewhere in France.
'Nigger, *what* you in jail fo'?'
              'Murder—'
                    'How long you's
gwine *be* in heah?'
        'Jes' three days.'
              'Why dat ain't fair,
nigger—you heah fo' murder, and dat's *all* you get?'
'Uh-huh—dey gwine hang me *Fri*day.'
              . . . Now all
you loafers, *sing*—Come *on*—'*I'm goin' to dance
off both my shoes, when they play the Jelly Roll Blues,
tomorrow night at the Darktown Strutters' Ba-a-all.*' "

MOLLIENS-AU-BOIS

MACHINE GUN EMPLACEMENT

"I'll be damned that's a Roman coin!"

"I been *tellin'* you so."

"Where d'you get it?"

"Well, it's the damdest you ever heard.
I bought it off of a guy 'n a machine gun crew
for five francs—I just heard about it today at mess.
They'd been diggin' away on the edge of the wood—you know
where the Hundred and Thirty-Second is? Some bird
comes along an' they're all playin' poker—'Gimme two—
what you bettin', ten coppers? I raise you twenty—I guess
I win, full house.' He asks where they got all the dough.
'I dug up a jar of it, sir.' He slips him a word
as to what the phoney stuff was. I'll give you a tip,
he's wise now, he's askin' ten francs."

"The dirty Jew—
Lemme see it. *A—U*—what's that—*C—AE—S*—
My God, think of using *that* for a poker chip!"

MOLLIENS-AU-BOIS

DIVISION HEADQUARTERS

"Say where d'you get all the candy?"
                            "Up at the Y."
"My God what's got into 'em?"
                    "You better go up there quick.
I had to stand a half an hour in line."
"Gimme some, you got lots."
                    "Say how do you get that way—
that belongs to the Major."
                        "O all right."

                                    Near by,
a piano jangles. In a field, the click
of pitching horseshoes—
                    "Whose turn is it?"
                                    "*Mine.*"
"What's that—O yes, the brigade goes in today."
Noon blazing blue gold in a summer sky
and helmets bobbing just above a thick
wheatfield, and through the dust of motorcars,
like streaks of rain the rifles slant and shine.
"Look there they go—"
                    "Yeh—Come on up, they say
the Y's got *cigarettes* and *Hershey* bars."

THE ROAD TO CORBIE

Our staff car flies and trails a long-spun haze
over the looping road and the surge and fall
of the heaving plains—quick dusty tree trunks throw
their flickering bars of shadow in our eyes.
A wood—men leading horses out to graze—
a misty bridge, and past the lumbering crawl
of crowded lorries—low hills all aglow
with tufts of trees against the evening skies
and long blond hill slopes catching level rays
along their quilted flanks—and under all,
the deep earth breathing like a thing asleep.
And there, Corbie—her brittle walls brought low—
a brick-choked wreck, in which her ruins rise
like gravestones planted in a rubbish heap.

CORBIE TO SAILLY-LE-SEC

High staggering walls, and plank-spiked piles of brick
and plaster—jagged gables wrenched apart,
and tall dolls' houses cleanly split in two—
Rooms gaping wide on every cloven floor,
pictures askew that made your throat go thick,
and humble furniture that tore your heart.
"By God let's get out of here!"
                                    We motored through
to the poplar marsh along the river's shore.
Sailly-le-Sec—her church one candlestick
on a broken altar, and beyond it, part
and a rounded apse—a dusty village husk
of rubble and tile. Low hills ahead, all blue,
and twinkling with the phosphorescent soar
of rockets leaping in the fringe of dusk.

CHIPILLY RIDGE

REGIMENTAL HEADQUARTERS

Steep prickly slopes in shadow from the moon
sagging behind us down the strident sky.
Guns blaze and slam. The stars burn fever bright.
A low white ridge ahead, and the crumpled sound
of shelling.

        "Jerry's out—"

                A snarling croon
wheels over us—quick glittering tracers fly
down a pale searchlight, and along the ground
bombs blast into smoky yellow shot with light.
"These runners will get you up there pretty soon.
—Take them up to the Second Battalion."

                    My tongue goes dry
and scrapy, and my lips begin to jerk—
—"Look out for the gas—they been pumping it in all night."
"Let's go, Tommy."
           "O God wait a minute—I've found
something wrong with my mask—the damn thing doesn't work."

CHIPILLY RIDGE

THROUGH THE VALLEY

"All right Tom?"

        "Yup—I got it fixed—let's start."

A slipping crumbly path through scratching brush
down to the river road. Along the shore
a clanging leap of fire behind black trees
and a streak of shrillness slit the sky apart.
A sand road—horses, guns in a cloudy rush,
and men, teeth clenched on tubes, who lashed and tore
through silence. Black still slopes—a distant sneeze.
"Hear that? I tell you—my eyes are beginning to smart."
A vague black gulch ahead, and the secret hush
of evil creeping in the dark—We passed
two soldiers, pain-white, and a man they bore
between, blind twisting head and drunken knees,
—like Christ.

        "Come on, Bud—There—You just been gassed."

CHIPILLY RIDGE

SECOND BATTALION HEADQUARTERS

"Where's the *First* Battalion? We haven't got any more
idea than *you* have—they might be anywhere.
There's no front line. You'll just get caught in a raid."

Cool darkness, after the foggy slobbering mask.
The long sky slashed with trundling swift uproar,
rumbling and husky in the whistling air,
and gas shells hustling into the valley made
a wobbling whisper like a hurtling flask.
We turned along the ridge to the river's shore.
"By God what's the matter with all those men?"
                                                    "*Hey* there—
excuse me, sir—you going by any chance
to the dressing station? I got twenty men—I'm afraid
they're gassed pretty bad—"
                              "What were you going to ask?"
"For God sake tell 'em to hurry up the ambulance."

CHIPILLY RIDGE

REGIMENTAL DRESSING STATION

Squat walls of sandbags—and above, a sky
all thin and cool with dawn and very far.
Black empty stretchers. On the parapet,
light out before the clangor of the gun.
The bliss of strong fatigue—and where I lie
the canvas breathes between me and that star
a bitter steam of blood. The air feels wet,
and the stars go, forgotten one by one.
Time to start back—and watch those towns go by!
"You ready to go?—we got a lift in a car."
"Already?—"
            "Yeh, let's start, we got a long way
to go."
            O God the ruins of Sailly-Laurette!
—like dying men that wake and find the sun
and shut their eyes against another day.

MOLLIENS-AU-BOIS

BRITISH CONCERT PARTY

Footlights and dancing, and the stage all gay
with Pierrot costumes white against a buff
backdrop of sacking—and the orchard strewn
with Yanks and Tommies taking in the show.
Strong voices ringing out—'*Down Texas way,
in the clover and the new-mown hay. . . .*'
                           "Aw *can* that stuff,
we *trained* in Texas!"
               Then a Hawaiian tune,
Yaaka Hula Hickey Dula, For Me and my Gal, and so
on—
    '*I wish I were in Dixie, Hooray, Hooray . . .*'
"O girls, look out if that fellow ever gets rough."
"Pipe down, you're spoiling the whole works, can't you see?"
Then all lights out—a full midsummer moon
in the apple trees, and a lanky wan Pierrot
sings slowly, '*Roses are shining in Picardy . . .*'

THE ROAD TO BAYONVILLERS

The sidecar skimmed low down like a flying sled
over the straight road with its double screen
of wire—the blue profile of Amiens sank
below the plain—near by, a hidden blast
of gunfire by the roadside—just ahead,
a white cloud bursting out of a slope of green.
Then low swift open land and the wasted flank
of a leprous hillside—over the ridge and past
the blackened stumps of Bois Vert, bleak and dead.
Our sidecar jolted and rocked, twisting between
craters, lunging at every rack and wrench.
Through Bayonvillers—her dusty wreckage stank
of rotten flesh, a dead street overcast
with a half-sweet, fetid, cloying fog of stench.

HARBONNIÈRES

REGIMENTAL MAPS FROM HEADQUARTERS

A dusty sunset in a smoky sky,
and soldiers idling over the dry terrain.
"Stop here—they're *some*where out by Harbonnières.
Give me the maps."
                              A rush of foaming flanks,
Australian caissons rattling, galloping by
and dust clouds sifting slowly on to the plain.
"You men seen any Americans anywhere?"
"No sir."
            "Wot's 'e want, we 'aven't seen any Yanks—"

"Seen an American regiment this way?"
                                          "Try
over there, Lieutenant—a mile or two off the main
road."

      —"Colonel, here are the maps."
                                    "What are *they* for?"
"For—distribution."
                      "With just one minute to spare
before we go up into line?—Well anyway, thanks—
They might be useful in another war."

HARBONNIÈRES TO BAYONVILLERS

PICNIC

A house marked 𝔒𝔯𝔱𝔰𝔨𝔬𝔪𝔪𝔞𝔫𝔡𝔞𝔫𝔱𝔲𝔯—a great
sign 𝕶𝖆𝖎𝖘𝖊𝖗𝖕𝖑𝖆𝖙𝖟 on a corner of the church,
and German street names all around the square.
Troop columns split to let our sidecar through.
"Drive like hell and get back on the main road—it's getting late."
"Yessir."
      The roadway seemed to reel and lurch
through clay wastes rimmed and pitted everywhere.
"You hungry?—Have some of this, there's enough for two."
We drove through Bayonvillers—and as we ate
men long since dead reached out and left a smirch
and taste in our throats like gas and rotten jam.
"Want any more?"
         "Yes sir, if you got enough there."
"Those fellows smell pretty strong."
         "I'll say they do,
but I'm too hungry sir to care a damn."

MOLLIENS-AU-BOIS

HEADQUARTERS TROOP KITCHEN

"Mess call!"

     "*Yea* Bo—"

          "Fall in, men—"

               "There she blows—"

"Say ain't you ready yet? You're slow as hell—"

—"Don't crowd around the kitchen!"

               —"*When* do we *eat!*

When do we *eat!*"

          —"Pipe down there! Hold out your kits—

One at a time!"

          —"The old slumgullion—"

               "Is those

baked beans again?"

          "Who buys us this Mirabelle?

My God what jam—"

          "I'm sick o' monkey meat—"

—"Quit griping you guys!"

          "He thinks he's a chef from the Ritz—"

—"Say what was the big fight?"

          "This drunken Australian goes

right up to the sentry—'You're an American—Well
I can lick every bleeding'—you know how they talk. Well that kike
of a bugler runs up—'You big Aussie, get t' Hell off our street'—
and gives him one poke in the jaw—You know Jake Horrowitz—"

"That runt? Can you *beat* that! Well for the love o' Mike—"

TRONVILLE-EN-BARROIS

NIGHT WATCH

Autumn and dusk—a band far off plays *I—*
*ain't got no*bo—*dy and* no*bo—dy cares for me.*
Already autumn here in this new part
of France—the garden has a bitter reek!
How lonely stars look in a changing sky—
I turn the lights on so as not to see.
Already late for my night watch to start.
Silence too strong for anything to creak.
The night is very wide—the room turns sly,
and things keep still to watch what there may be
back of my tight shut eyes and secret smile.
Are you there?—and like the heart of God my heart
is vast with love and pain and very bleak—
O France, be still in here a little while.

BLERCOURT

LA VOIE SACRÉE

These houses died too long ago to care
who comes and echoes in their empty shells.
Our broken rooms stay blank and vacant still
although we laughed and talked an hour or two.
Rats squeak and scrabble brusquely everywhere.
The night is almost blind . . . Something dispels
my stupor, wakes me with a squeamish thrill
to find my raincoat pocket eaten through . . .
How can I sleep with Verdun over there!
Once out of doors, what is it breaks and wells
to tears,—just to be marching along the grey
of the road, with Verdun back of any hill,
Verdun, in touch and sentient—there to view
my lonely crisis on her sacred way.

FROMERÉVILLE

IN A DUGOUT

Sleep ripped apart in the shrilling blast of a shell
jerking me back into life—Dawn, and a dead
bleak silence split by a shrieking smash—one then,
every minute! Men run along the corridor—
"Say look in here."
        "It's the General's—"
                "Naw it's too swell,
it's the Billeting Officer's—look at the real brass bed—"
"Not so loud!"
        "They're asleep—"
            A shadowy press of men
and tilted helmets at the open door.
My body swept throughout with a shattering spell
of fear—the fear that makes your heart like lead
your gullet sicken and the bowels creep
and slide like live things in your abdomen.
"Olly wake up!"
        "Hey!—what did you wake me for?
Aw Hell, why this is nothing—go to sleep."

FROMEREVILLE

PARTY

A drift of sunlight in the upper air.
The shallow valley is already grey.
Dusk settles in the dingy village street,
and no birds gather in the empty skies.
Mess call!—another from beyond the square.
"Is Tommy back from Bar-le-Duc?"
                              "I'll say
he is and with the swellest things to eat!
Here try that."
            "Pass the liquor, damn your eyes."
"Tonight's the Troop's big party."
                              "Let's go there—
your friend the M. P. sergeant's going to play.
Listen!"
            . . . *'Ashes to ashes and dust to dust'* . . .
and as we crowd in, laughter, and the beat
of voice and piano as the riot dies
away—*'If the whiskey don't get you then the cocaine must'* . . .

FROMEREVILLE

WAR IN HEAVEN

A reek of steam—the bath-house rang with cries.
"Come across with the soap."
                    "Like hell, what makes you think
it's yours?"
          "Don't turn *off the water*, that ain't fair
I'm all *covered* with soap."
                    "Hurry up, get out of the way."
"Thank God you're takin' a bath."
                    "He wants to surprise
us."
     "Oh is that so, well anyway I don't stink
like you."
          "Air raid!"
                    We ran out into the square,
naked and cold like souls on Judgment Day.
Over us, white clouds blazoned on blue skies,
and a green balloon on fire—we watched it shrink
into flame and a fall of smoke. Around us, brute
guns belching puffs of shrapnel in the air,
where one plane swooping like a bird of prey
spat fire into a dangling parachute.

FORT DE LANDRECOURT

ABOVE VERDUN

An autumn ridge of dun and rust and slate—
and low green banks along a wet grey sky.
Deep walls and bastions in a moat of grass.
S'ENSEVELIR SOUS LES RUINES DU FORT
PLUTOT QUE DE SE RENDRE—above the gate.
My horse clatters on to the drawbridge, and a shy
young sentry smiles and will not let me pass.
"On ne visite pas?"
                                "Sans permission?—alors,
je le regrette"—we grin and separate.
Verdun below—where all those ruins lie.
And in my heart a love that almost kills
to see her, gashed and militant—a mass
of wreckage crying out "Debout les morts"
to all the souls that haunt her tragic hills.

LEMPIRE

ENTENTE CORDIALE

"You ready, Joe?"

    "Yessir."

        —"Messieurs, à table!

Ici, mon commandant."

    "That's right, you tell 'em where,

we none of us savvy their lingo."

        —"Voilà, messieurs."

"Who paint thees card? 'Tis 'ow you say, a *peach*—

de eagle shake 'and weet de coc—C'est admirable!"

"Where's the *soup* Joe—*What?* Which wine first? We don't care,

get 'em tight as quick as you can."

        "Ils sont fameux

ces Américains, avec leurs bouteilles!"

        "*We*'ll teach

'em to drink."

    "Mais qu'est-ce que c'est qu'*ça?*—C'est *formidable!*"

"My God Joe, you served all four courses at once!"

        "Hey there—

speech, Commaundaunt."

    "I regrette not to speak."

"Come on there Skipper, it's your turn—Give 'em a speech."

"Bottoms up, men!"

    "A la santé des deux

républiques!"

    "Yea—*Vive* la *France!*"

        "Vive l'*Amérique!*"

LEMPIRE

HEADQUARTERS TROOP BARRACKS

"Aw Sunny France—ain't this a hell of a day,
nothin' but rain and rain—"
                    "Jest mark mah word,
they'll have us out there diggin' a new latrine."
"It must be swell to be on the General's staff
and just have bright ideas!"

                    —"Say keep away
from that girl at Landrecourt, from what *I* heard—"

—"This outfit's got the best you ever seen—
you don't know a thing about horses and that ain't the half—"
"The hell I don't."
                    "Aw run along and play—
why you can't tell a horse from a cockeyed bird—"

"Roll them bones—"
                    "Come on now—couple of twos—"
"Come on there, box cars—"
                    "Crap there—give us that *mean*
seven—*Hot* damn—honest I have to laugh."
"Come on you snake eyes—Baby wants a *new* pair o' shoes."

LEMPIRE

SOUVENIRS

Our supper broke up at a burst of cheers—
"Say what the hell goes on—"
                            —"*Hey* Captain *Styles!*"
We tumbled out.
            —"He's landed!"
                        "Gee he got
that Jerry swell."
            "Come on!"
                        Across the yard
we ran, and the bridge by the Engineers,
then uphill—over into the valley for miles
it seemed through bog and brush at a dead trot
into the dark wood, half sick, gasping hard.
Around the burnt plane, raking souvenirs,
a crowd, all raucous shouts and breathless smiles—
"Hey quit your shoving there."
                        —"I'll say she did."
—It's his first Heinie."
                        —"*Jesus Christ* that's hot!"
—"I *seen* the bastard, *sure*—he's under guard—
sixteen—he's nothing but a goddam *kid!*"

SOUILLY

HOSPITAL

Fever, and crowds—and light that cuts your eyes—
Men waiting in a long slow-shuffling line
with silent private faces, white and bleak.
Long rows of lumpy stretchers on the floor.
My helmet drops—a head jerks up and cries
wide-eyed and settles in a quivering whine.
The air is rank with touching human reek.
A troop of Germans clatters through the door.
They cross our line and something in me dies.
Sullen, detached, obtuse—men into swine—
and hurt unhappy things that walk apart.
Their rancid bodies trail a languid streak
so curious that hate breaks down before
the dull and cruel laughter in my heart.

HOSPITAL TRAIN

Sick fretful upper berths—below, long rows
of faces with the same young stricken eyes.
Blind smoke, and the restless shift of awkward legs
and stiff clean bandages too thick for blood.
"Where's this car going?"
                        "Angers."
                              —"Wha'd he say?"
                                          "God knows,
some frog dump."
                  —"Hold that match, thanks."
                                    —"Any o' you guys
got a Lucky?"
              —"Say listen, this buddy of mine . . ."
                                                —"I pegs
away at the cap. I thought it was a dud."
—"*Oh!*"
        "God I'm sorry Buddy."
                        —"Say you Bos,
what would you give for some good old apple pies
'like your mother used to bake'—"
                          "Don't make us blue!"
"And *watermelon*—"
                "And *corn*—"
                        "And *ham an' eggs*—"
—"Hey, look up there."
                "Where was you wounded, Bud?"
"Aw I'm not wounded Buddy—it's just the flu."

finee
la
guerre

GLOSSARY

abri	underground shelter
Archies	Anti-Aircraft guns
Attaboy! . . .	That's the boy!
Aussies	Australians
Banyuls	a red wine from the Pyrenees
bavarder . . .	chatter
bear	champion
billet	assigned lodging
Bo, bos	derived from bozo, fellow or guy
box cars	a throw of twelve at dice
bunkie	pal
Byrrh	a widely advertized apéritif or appetizer
cave	cellar
cockeyed . . .	drunk, also equivalent to damned
crap ; . . .	a throw of seven at dice
crever	to be all in, drop with fatigue
"Debout les morts!"	the cry of a dying French soldier who thereby rallied about him all his desperately wounded comrades and led them to victory
dud	a shell which has landed without exploding
fine	cognac, *fine champagne*
G-2	Second Section of the General Staff in charge of Military Intelligence
hayseed	farmer
Hershey bar . .	a chocolate and almond bar
hick	bumpkin
Jerry	another name for Heinie or Fritz
kike	Jew

liaison	communication maintained between units
lorry	British truck
Lulu	prize-winner
M. P.	Military Police
Mairie . . .	Town Hall
Mercerie . . .	Dry goods store
mirabelle . . .	plum jam
monkey-meat . .	tinned beef, Corn Willy
Ordnance . . .	Corps in charge of ammunition
Orts-Kommandantur	Town Major's office
outfit	organization, unit
patois	local dialect
pipe down . . .	quiet down
Quincaillerie . .	Hardware store
Red Tabs . . .	Officers of the British General Staff
Riley	to lead the life of Riley is to be in absolute luxury and ease
S'ENSEVELIR, etc.	Let the fort bury you under its ruins rather than surrender.
slumgullion . . .	meat and vegetable stew
snake-eyes . . .	a throw of ones at dice
step on it . . .	be quick about it
tracer	a machine-gun bullet with a pyrotechnic device to render visible its trajectory
la Voie Sacrée . .	The road from Bar-le-Duc to Verdun which served to support Verdun after the destruction of the railway between that city and Sainte-Menehould